Sacred Sabbath

Sacred Sabbath

God's way to multiply our time and restore our joy

THE TEN COMMANDMENTS SERIES

Marja Verschoor-Meijers

Dedication

My husband and I would like to dedicate this book to the Swift family, who always supported us and made our residency in California possible.

The Lord says, "If you treat the Sabbath as sacred and do not pursue your own interests on that day; if you value my holy day and honor it by not traveling, working, or talking idly on that day, then you will find the joy that comes from serving me. I will make you honored all over the world, and you will enjoy the land I gave to your ancestor, Jacob. I, the Lord, have spoken."

Isaiah 58:13-14

Table of contents

Foreword

When I first read Marja's book 'Sacred Sabbath', I literally had no idea how profound the impact of this manuscript would be. Even though I have pastored a church and been in ministry for over 20 years, I found myself receiving new insights and principles to approach the Sabbath. Her style of writing and accuracy of Scripture immediately started to quench a thirst inside of me as I read each page. It was so enlightening that I read the book in one sitting.

I believe this book is loaded with life changing nuggets. Marja's low-key, down-to-earth style helps the reader become very comfortable, as if you were sitting down having a cup of coffee or tea with her. I believe she is a fresh voice and a much needed one. Over the years, I have seen Marja grow into a woman of impeccable faith. I have had the privilege of having lunch with her and her husband, Jan, and they both made a great impact on my life. What she writes in this book, she lives. I believe her being relaxed, easy-going, never in a hurry, always having time for friends and family, and yet found time to write this powerful book is a testimony to how special she is.

My wife, Kimberly, and I have always felt she was destined to do big things. This book is just one of the many big and impactful things she will accomplish with her life. If you are serious about change, this book will help mentor you in a way that you have never dreamed of. I believe it is one that will help you reach a fulfilled life.

If you read it, your eyes will be opened to a new level of living, a new level of peace that comes only when you see the Sabbath as sacred.

Pastor Lonnie G. McCowan D.D.J.D.
Ventura, CA (2005)

Introduction

Then God commanded, "Let lights appear in the sky to separate day from night and to show the time when days, years, and religious festivals [or: seasons] begin..."

Genesis 1:14

One sunny morning, back in August 2004, my husband and I were sitting at the breakfast table in our home in Southern California. We were studying the Bible and praying, when somehow we came across Isaiah 58:13-14. I heard an unmistakable voice inside my spirit: 'This is your book.'

Just that simple, just that short. Nothing less, nothing more. A few years prior to that moment I had given my life to Jesus and it was the first time I heard His voice and it startled me a bit. Not because He encouraged me to write a book, but because I heard it so clearly. Like many would-be writers and authors, I had wanted to write a book since I was a child.

Even at a young age I just loved the written word. I published my own handwritten magazine when I was about eight years old and distributed it among my friends. The love for the written word was expressed in my involvement in school publications, church flyers, business news letters, etc.

Writing travel diaries, short stories, and even a poem here and there, was more than a hobby; it turned out to be my passion. However, a real fresh idea, something worth publishing for a greater public, never came up.

Looking back, it is easy to see how God gave me the ability to write (first of all in my own language, Dutch) and many opportunities to practice. That natural talent combined with spiritual giftings I received when I became a believer, took writing to a whole new level. In the church my husband and I attended at the time, the Solid Rock Christian Center in Ventura, we had received a teaching about open doors and opportunities.

Being in the internship program of that church, the pastor promised us at the beginning of the 2004 semester the necessary motivational and practical support in case any of us wanted to write and publish a book. Right there and them, it came to my mind: 'This is my chance.' Still, I had a hundred excuses not to start right away. What topic? Will people read it? I don't have a computer, etc.

That one morning at the breakfast table, between toast and coffee, the door opened for the real thing, the real work. I wrote the words, as found in Isaiah 58:13-14, on a piece of paper and we immediately prayed over those verses. We thanked God for the book idea, we prayed for wisdom and inspiration, we blessed the work of my hands, and we declared it a bestseller before one word had been written. Well, you do have to dream big, don't you? The book was there in the spiritual; it was my job to give it form in the natural.

When God wants work to be done, He has it all figured out long before we realize what is happening. I began to see the true value of the words in Ephesians 2:10,

God has made us what we are, and in our union with Christ Jesus he has created us for a life of good deeds, which he has already prepared for us to do.

He provided the idea, the inspiration, the support, and even the tools. A dear brother and sister from our church in The Netherlands came to visit us in Southern California and blessed us with a brand new laptop. It seemed everything was prepared, but the labor itself. When things line up as I just described, there are no more excuses, there is work to do.

When God has a message for His people, He uses someone to proclaim it. He uses a messenger, a prophet, a voice, or a writer. Often someone who has no clue as of what to say or how to explain things. In my case, someone who did not even master the language perfectly, someone who had never written a book before, and someone who had never spoken to an entire generation. Besides such practical issues, the topic of sabbatical rest had never been on my mind.

Well, up until the day He spoke so clearly to my heart about penning down what this book would be about. I had never thought about keeping the Sabbath although I grew up in a Christian home where Sunday, the first day of the week, was considered a day set apart for God and church.

I had never thought about the importance of the Sabbath until my husband and I came to the USA and noticed that there was not even room for a Sabbath in the American 24/7 society. The term 'a day of rest' had disappeared, even within Christian circles. We regarded that phenomenon as a cultural issue, until the Lord spoke to me about writing this book.

The message it holds is not deep or complicated, but rather spiritual revelation. It is His message, and I see it as my assignment to share it with the hope and intention that it will make us all re-think His Word, our lives, and the direction we are going, Maybe even the direction our nation is going.

If you are curious and ready to receive an uncommon thought, I urge you to pray this prayer before you start reading. It will help you to open your heart and mind for the Spirit to speak to you!

Dear Father in Heaven, I honor You and I honor Your Word. I thank You for Your everlasting love for me. Holy Spirit, help me to open up my mind and heart for this

message. I want to fulfill God's Word by living it! I pray
this in Jesus' name. Amen.

Marja Verschoor-Meijers

Sab-bath (sab th),*n.*[ME. *sabat* < OFr. & AS. *sabat;*
both , L. *sabbatum;* Gr. *sabaton;* Heb. *shabb th* < *sh*
bath, to rest], 1. The seventh day of the Jewish week, set
aside by the fourth Commandment for rest and worship;
Saturday. 2. Sunday: name applied by most Protestant
denominations. 3. [s-], a period of rest. *Adj.* of the
Sabbath. Abbreviated **S., Sab.**

Statement

Before we begin our journey through this book, it is important to take notice of the following statement. As the title of this book suggests, this is a book about the Sabbath and keeping it holy. This is *not* a book about rules. The Bible says in Colossians 2:16-17,

So let <u>no one</u> make rules about what you eat or drink or about holy days or the New Moon Festival or the Sabbath. All such things are only a shadow of things in the future; the reality is Christ.

Let no one make rules, but God of course! For He alone is Lord of the Sabbath. Throughout the centuries people did make rules though. The Jewish leaders did it, the church did it, and my parents did it as you will read further on in this book. We will dive into this. One thing, however, is clear: the seventh day of the week is called Sabbath (Saturday). That is still so, that will never change. No discussion needed. Although the Bible calls the Sabbath a day of rest, Jesus entered the synagogue on the Sabbath and taught (Mark 1:21 and Mark 6:2 for example). So much for a day of rest.

After the Sabbath, the first day of the week begins (Sunday) as stated in Matthew 28:1. The disciples and other believers assembled on the first day of the week

(John 20:19 and Acts 20:7). This is still the custom of many believers today. Some travel far to be in such a meeting. So much for a day of rest. I mean, if you minister to a congregation on Saturday or on Sunday for example, you know how intense and tiring that can be. You will definitely need another day of rest, which can be any day of the week.

Although God declared the seventh day a day of rest for His people, as we can read in the fourth commandment, it is also true that things have changed somewhat under the New Covenant. Paul writes in Romans 14:5,

Some people think that a certain day is more important than other days, while others think that all days are the same. We each should firmly make up our own minds.

When we read that verse in the context, we will discover that this is about living for God, not about following certain rules. So, please, set aside any religious, rigid ideas and receive revelation from the Holy Spirit about the spiritual concept of a 'holy day', such as the Sabbath.

This book holds a simple but clear message from the Holy Spirit which I addressed to Christians in America at first. But now, so many years later, I realize the message is for the universal body of Christ all over the world. May it be a blessing and encouragement to you.

So, which day of the week is your day of rest is of no importance to the message that I want to bring across in this book. The main point to be made is the blessing that will follow when we take a day of rest after six days of work. I realize this may sound revolutionary to some and liberating to others. This book is not a promotion for a holy Saturday or for a holy Sunday. I leave that discussion up to others. This book is about the deeper spiritual truth behind the fourth commandment and the way we can live according to that truth in our daily lives.

4th Commandment

Observe the Sabbath and keep it holy. You have six days in which to do your work, but the seventh day is a day of rest dedicated to me. On that day no one is to work— neither you, your children, your slaves, your animals, nor the foreigners who live in your country. In six days I, the Lord, made the earth, the sky, the seas, and everything in them, but on the seventh day I rested. That is why I, the Lord, blessed the Sabbath and made it holy.

Exodus 20:8-11

Part I

The Lord says, "If you treat the Sabbath as sacred and do not pursue your own interests on that day; if you value my holy day and honor it by not traveling, working, or talking idly on that day..."

Isaiah 58:13

1

When God speaks

Listen, then, if you have ears!

Matthew 13:9

That morning in August 2004, when the Lord spoke to me, changed my life forever. It marked the official beginning of my writing journey. I had been writing ever since I was a child, but never before had I heard the voice of the Lord so clearly, and so specifically. Ever since that morning I must have read the passage in Isaiah 58:13-14, which is the basis for the book you are holding, a hundred times.

We will go through that passage step by step and I hope you will notice how rich and powerful these verses are. Let's start by exploring verse 13, a rather long verse.

<u>The Lord says,</u> *"If you treat the Sabbath as_sacred and do not pursue your own interests on that day; if you value my holy day and honor it by not traveling, working, or talking idly on that day..."*

This verse is a direct message from God to the reader, to you and me, and it opens up with the words: 'The Lord says…' May I urge you to stop right there. Maybe it is not the common way to start a book by asking readers to stop and think a while about the first sentence, but then, this book is not about the common way.

It is of great importance to sit down, take time, and think for a while about the true meaning behind a little sentence like that. 'The Lord says', implies the spoken word. God speaks a word and when He speaks, He creates. It is up to us whether we want to pay attention or not. When God speaks, He creates, He brings something into existence, just as He created light by using words. We can find praise for His creating power in Psalms 148. The writer of that psalm urges all creation to glorify God as we can see in verses 2-5,

Praise him, all his angels, all his heavenly armies. Praise him, sun and moon; praise him, shining stars. Praise him, highest heavens, and the waters above the sky. Let them all praise the name of the Lord! He commanded, and they were created.

He commanded, and they were created. That is the reason for this worship. God created more than the heavens and the earth. He spoke laws, promises, and truths into existence. These are all written down in His Word for the reader to meditate on and live by.

Notice that Isaiah 58:13-14 is written in present tense and that He addresses you, me, us. Please, do not read this with the word 'history' all over it. We should read it as if God is giving us the message today.

God speaks throughout the entire Bible in various ways. In the Old Testament He speaks through the leaders of Israel, through prophets, angels, and, believe it or not, a donkey (see the story in Numbers 22 if you are curious). In the New Testament God speaks through angels, His Son Jesus, and the apostles. In Matthew 24:35 the importance and power of God's words are made clear in a strong statement of Jesus,

Heaven and earth will pass away, but my words will never pass away.

God's words are eternal and of eternal value. On many occasions, Jesus told His disciples about the importance of His words, which were of course the words He received from His Father. He spoke divine words with power and authority. In John 7:16 for example, Jesus declares:

What I teach is not my own teaching, but it comes from God, who sent me.

In this 21st century God still speaks. He speaks to us through His written Word, the Bible. Yes, He also speaks through His Holy Spirit, but first and foremost through

His Word. Whether you read the Bible regularly, hardly ever open it up, or never read a word, does not change the message of the Bible. Some people might not read it, but millions and millions of people all over the world do, and they do so in more than seven hundred languages! As a matter of fact, more and more people start reading the Bible in an ongoing quest to find answers to life's problems, challenges, and questions.

This could be a good moment to pick up a Bible translation that truly speaks to your age and generation and give it a try. In this book, I have purposely used, unless otherwise noted, the Good News Translation (GNT) formerly known as the Today's English Version (TEV). I like that version because it really opened my eyes for the scriptures with its simple, down-to-earth, yet powerful style. Since English is not my native language, not my mother tongue, I need clear and simple words in order to understand what I am reading. Picking up the Good News Translation changed everything I had ever heard or learned before.

Let me ask you a straightforward question: 'Do you believe that the Bible is God's Word and do you want to take His Word seriously?' Be honest when you think this over. We might have a tendency to only take seriously what appeals to us or what we think is useful and easily applicable in life. We reason that to be able to take every word seriously, we need divine thinking and God's wisdom flowing through us at all times.

In other words, we like to use our humanity as an excuse to take from His Word what we like and what is understandable and to ignore the passages we struggle with or that do not seem to fit in our modern-day society. We like to regard these passages as mere history or theory, which is a shame if you ask me.

We have to look into God's Word to find keys we can use to change our way of thinking. The apostle Paul was a great scholar and thinker, no doubt. After he had an encounter with Jesus, he understood that his own intellect and thinking were limited and that he was in need of divine help. In 1 Corinthians 2:16b we can read one of his most powerful conclusions,

We, however, have the mind of Christ.

What made Paul say that? Can we as Christians, as followers of Jesus, truly have the mind of Christ? I believe with Paul that we can. By reading the Bible we learn to think His thoughts. And why do I believe so? Because Jesus explained why and how that is possible for His followers. Let's take a look at His words in John 15:15 (NIV),

I no longer call you servants, because a servant does not know his master's business. Instead, I have called you

friends, for everything that I learned from my Father I have made known to you.

Through Jesus everything was made known to us. What an awesome truth, let it sink in for a moment. Everything was made known to us, that is, if we accept His friendship. He calls us His friends. He never said we couldn't be. His offer still stands today, He has not changed His mind. His invitation is simple, all we have to do is decide whether we want to accept His invitation to become His friend as well.

Meditate on the following:

- *Am I willing to believe that the whole Bible is God's Word?*
- *Can I truly say that I am a friend of Jesus?*

Journal your thoughts:

2

A personal friend

But that is not all; we rejoice because of what God has done through our Lord Jesus Christ, who has now made us God's friends.

Romans 5:11

'All we have to do is decide whether we want to accept His invitation to become His friend as well.' Did I make that sound too simple? Maybe. It is possible you never thought about becoming friends with Jesus. Well, it does not really matter that these words were spoken two thousand years ago; they are still valid today.

If we want to be a part of Jesus' circle of friends, all we have to do is make a conscious decision to turn away from doing our own will and embrace doing His will. It starts by saying out loud that Jesus is Lord and by believing in our heart that God raised Him from death. I know, it sounds easy indeed. Surely, there has to be more to embracing a friendship with God Himself? What about forgiveness of sins and all that? Listen, we are forgiven,

Jesus already paid the price for the sins of the whole world. It is up to every individual to accept that or not. Yes, the Bible tells us to stop our sinful ways and to turn our lives into another direction. Saying out loud that Jesus is Lord is not just a simple statement. It means that sin is no longer lord in our lives. It means that we will obey God and no longer our own desires. It means a major shift in our lives, in the direction we are going.

A shift, a turning point, that we will never regret. If we are honest about our confession of faith, it will work for us. We should all underline Romans 10:9-10 in our Bibles if we haven't done so already.

If you confess that Jesus is Lord and believe that God raised him from death, you will be saved. For it is by our faith that we are put right with God; it is by our confession that we are saved.

Saying out loud (and meaning it) that Jesus is Lord will change our lives forever. Aren't you glad we don't have to jump through hoops, prepare a speech, do a qualification test, or get a goofy haircut (not to talk about paying a membership fee) to be part of Jesus' circle of friends?

As we have read in chapter one, everything was made known to us through Jesus. So, if there are things we do not understand or grasp yet, don't worry. The longer we hang out with Him, the longer we are His friends, the more we read His words, the more we will see things become clear. Do not worry about the lack of knowledge or lack of understanding. The Bible will turn out to be a never-ending source of information, wisdom, revelation, and personal teaching. God is not a mysterious God somewhere far away on His own safe planet. He made Himself *known* to us throughout the Old Testament and then, in what we call the New Testament, He sent His Son Jesus to earth to make Himself *visible*, to be an example.

It didn't stop there. Jesus was crucified for our sins and sicknesses and was raised from the dead on the third day to sit again at the right-hand side of God. After that, God has sent the Holy Spirit to live inside believers so they can still communicate with the Father and the Son. In John 14:26 Jesus says,

The Helper, the Holy Spirit, whom the Father will send in my name, will teach you everything and make you remember all that I have told you.

Never be discouraged.

I wrote all this to put emphasis on the fact that God's Word is for us today. It is just as powerful today as it was in ancient times. In Hebrews 4:12 (NIV) it is written,

For the word of God is alive and active. Sharper than any double-edged sword...

He wants us to read it, believe it, do it, live it, and spread it. The Word is as applicable today as it was thousands of years ago. It speaks to individuals in a present tense. It will speak to whoever is willing to hear and understand at any given moment. A great exercise to make the Bible more personal is to fill in our own name, wherever possible, when reading. The words of Jesus in John 14:26, as we just read them, would sound like this: 'The Helper, the Holy Spirit, whom the Father will send in my name, will teach Marja everything and make Marja remember all that I have told her.'

When reading the Word out loud and filling in our own name, we can actually hear God speak, although it is our own voice, we are speaking His words. No longer do we need to say, 'I cannot hear God. I do not understand Him. I never hear His voice.' His voice is written down for all generations. It truly helps to read it out loud and personalize it.

God speaks to us in ways we can never imagine. His Word truly comes to life at our dining room table, at our computer desk, in the living room, in the back yard, on the beach, or in the mountains, or wherever we study and listen. Whenever we want or need to hear from Him, we can simply open up His Word, read aloud and listen!

The Lord says…

Meditate on the following:

- *Do I truly realize that God can speak to me personally through His written Word? Do I dare to fill in my own name where possible?*
- *How do I value the Bible from a historical, literal, and moral perspective?*

Journal your thoughts:

3

Our busy lives

I find pleasure in obeying your commands, because I love them. I respect and love your commandments; I will meditate on your instructions.

Psalm 119:47-48

God speaks to us when we read Isaiah 58:13-14. He speaks to us personally, but He also speaks to a nation that reads His Word. Today, He speaks to us, to a generation that is struggling with stress, too little time to get everything done, and the ever-present feeling that life is slipping through our hands. Let's continue to study Isaiah 58:13.

The Lord says, "If you treat the Sabbath as sacred and do not pursue your own interests on that day; if you value my holy day and honor it by not traveling, working, or talking idly on that day..."

I believe God has given us clear guidelines to prevent a frustrating kind of living. He makes us an offer we cannot and should not refuse. He wants us to have a day of rest after every six days of working, a day dedicated to Him, a day that we treat as sacred (set apart from other days). A day with great blessings attached, as we will see further on.

We may ask how God knew where we would end up in the 21st century. Did He already know that we would be running out of time? Did He truly foresee that stress, anxiety, burn-outs, and depression would be almost incurable diseases in our modern-day society? Is that why He warned us beforehand? Is that why He gave us the principle of a day of rest after every six days of work?

Do you know where we will end up with questions like these? We will end up in the Bible. God did indeed foresee our troubles. That is why He gave us clear guidelines, solid orders, and simple laws. That is why He counseled us before we even asked for help. That is why He has given us a manual when He assembled our lives, so to speak.

He has given us inside knowledge on how to avoid stress (and many more things besides that). Our problem is that we find it so hard to understand the language, as in the manual that comes with a new television set or washing machine. We rather skip the manual simply because it takes too much time and effort to read all the instructions. That is often how we handle God's Word.

We are sometimes reluctant to let God speak into our lives. We often interrupt Him after reading the first sentence of a chapter. 'Oh God, don't give us that. Don't burden us with religious stuff. We really don't need to be told what to do and what not to do. We are grown-ups.' Yes, so often we are afraid God wants to burden us with rules and regulations. That is the last thing we need; we want to be free!

Haven't we all been there at some time in our lives? We are proud of our independent lives and our self-supportiveness. Yes, we are even proud of all the self-help books we have read and the pages with truly useful advice we have found on the internet. We know our way around this world. We know all about time management and multi-tasking. We have become masters in planning and scheduling.

Who doesn't have a full calendar page each week on the refrigerator door or a full digital agenda in our phones or a weekly schedule at the office? Wherever we go, our hours seem to be planned by others: opening and closing hours in the stores, office hours at the bank and government offices, class schedules at the gym or university, appointments openings at the doctor's office, etc. etc. Our days are filled from morning till evening. We have arrived, haven't we?

I know I speak for many when I make the statement that somehow the big questions still remain: 'If we are all so busy moving, what are we headed toward? Where are we going? Are we able to define our destination? Why the rush? When are we supposed to arrive?' If we are so capable of running our own lives, how come we end up tired, stressed out, overwhelmed, and sometimes even depressed? The biggest and most frustrating question of all might be this one: 'How come we hardly ever get the feeling that we are where we want to be?' Where did we go wrong?

Oh, if we would only take some time to listen. Someone wants to talk with us. Someone has wanted to talk with us for a long, long time. God knows our busy lives, our hectic schedules, and our longing for some rest and peace of mind. He knew. He knew all along. That is why He wants to talk with us about time, about the days that make up a week, about the weeks that make up a year, and the years that make up our lives.

Many people doubt whether the God of the Old Testament has the answers for our problems today. After all, it was a different time and it seems that people were spending their precious time fighting violent wars, setting up camp, watering their gardens, and maybe counting cattle. No sight yet of a 24/7 society, weekend jobs, endless social obligations, frequent credit problems that take up time and effort, and on top of that sport games, new movies, and Netflix series to watch every week.

Will the God of Abraham, Isaac, and Jacob be able to help us today to live a happy, balanced, and peaceful life? The answer is yes. He is as serious about guiding us today as He was about guiding His beloved people thousands of years ago. The real question is, do we want to hear what He has to say? Are we open to suggestions?

Meditate on the following:

- *Am I ready to believe that I need a day of rest after every six-day work period?*
- *Am I willing to dedicate that day to the Lord?*

Journal your thoughts:

4

Sacred Sabbath

But now you have been set free from sin and are the slaves of God. Your gain is a life fully dedicated to him, and the result is eternal life.

Romans 6:22

When reading the first part of Isaiah 58:13 we will notice that God starts with the word 'if'. He is not commanding. He is not asking. He is not warning. The way I personally read it is as if He is trying to make a deal with me. If you do this and this…

The Lord says, "If you treat the Sabbath as sacred and do not pursue your own interests on that day; if you value my holy day and honor it by not traveling, working, or talking idly on that day…"

He does not yell or bark His orders. He merely wants to give us help to live our daily lives. I do know enough of God's ways to realize that when He says 'if', He is serious in teaching me a principle, a law, a lesson. If He starts like that, He has my full attention and I hope He has yours too! Verse 13 starts with a proposal. Let's say we do not know what comes next, we do not know what the second part of this scripture is. Let us just concentrate on this particular sentence in Isaiah 58:13,

If you treat the Sabbath as sacred...

First of all, God speaks about the Sabbath here. We have to go to the fourth of the Ten Commandments to learn more about the Sabbath. Only the second and fourth commandments are considerably longer than the rest. More words are needed to describe the commandments about the prohibiting of idol worship and keeping the Sabbath holy than were needed for the other eight. This fact shows me that God is serious about the Sabbath. In Exodus 20:8-10a it is written,

Observe the Sabbath and keep it holy. You have six days in which to do your work, but the seventh day is a day of rest dedicated to me.

It goes on from there with instructions and explanations regarding that special day. As I wrote in the statement at the beginning of this book, the Biblical Sabbath day is the seventh day of the week (Saturday) and it is still being observed in Israël and by Jews all over the world. Apart from this weekly highlight, other Jewish feasts in the Bible are often called Sabbath days as well, implying they are holy days.

Now, personally, I don't think gentile believers are called to keep those days, simply because we do not live in Israel and we are not Jewish. We should not ask people to keep the holy days and at the same time we should not criticize people who do keep them. We are free to make up our own minds, as the apostle Paul wrote in Romans 14:5-7 (NKJV),

One person considers one day more sacred than another; another considers every day alike. Each of them should be fully convinced in their own mind. Whoever regards one day as special does so to the Lord. Whoever eats meat does so to the Lord, for they give thanks to God; and whoever abstains does so to the Lord and gives thanks to God. For none of us lives for ourselves alone, and none of us dies for ourselves alone.

The principle of having a sabbath day, however, is very important and meant to be a blessing in our lives. Whether that day is Saturday, Sunday or any other day of the week is not important as long as we are fully convinced in our own minds. If the Holy Spirit prompts you to keep the Saturday Sabbath, please do so. Dedicate that day to the Lord but keep in mind that under the New Covenant it is more important to understand the spiritual core value of rest than it is to legalistically be a Sabbath keeping believer.

The point of view that I have taken in this book is that after every six days of work God wants us to establish a day of rest. In that way the week becomes a cycle that repeats itself, starting from a position of rest. Not just an ordinary day of rest though, He wants us to dedicate that day to Him. Now, you might be thinking: 'Oh my goodness, being a Christian is already a full-time job, it is a lifestyle really. Does God want more?' Yes, He wants it all. Jesus says in Matthew 10:39 (NIV),

Whoever finds their life will lose it, and whoever loses their life for my sake will find it.

Yes, He wants all of our time, our whole life, everything. At the same time, He promises something in return. God wants us to have more. He wants to help us by giving specific guidelines for this special, sacred day.

He wants us to recognize a Sabbath day, a day of rest after every six days of work. He wants us to treat that day as sacred. Sacred means 'to set apart'. He wants that day to be different from the rest of our days. Unmistakably different. Don't worry yet as on how to fill that in; God gives us tips and advice. Let us concentrate on the first part of this scripture where God starts to set up His deal with us. I want to be sure that we meditate on this part of Isaiah 58:13, not just read it and forget it.

In a sense, I want us to set aside the rules and regulations we may have adapted when growing up, at least while reading this book. Not that certain habits and customs are necessarily wrong, but we need to open up to a new way of thinking. When we set aside what we may already know about God's holy day or about the so-called 'Lord's day' we grew up with, we create room to receive fresh insights on ancients truths. I want us to think about what God is going to offer. He wants to make an offer we cannot refuse. Are we ready for that?

To continue on to the next part of our foundation scripture, we need to make up our minds concerning two things God talks about, when He says: *'If you treat the Sabbath as sacred... '*

The first one: We need a Sabbath (a day of rest) every seventh day. After all, if Almighty God wanted rest after working six days, what makes us think we can do without? We are made in His image, aren't we? I am sure God didn't need the rest; He is God! However, I understand He wanted to set an example for generations to come. When God created the whole universe, He designed everything very carefully.

We only need to look around at mountains, deserts, oceans, a tiny butterfly, a giant lion, and at people with their unique characters. Not a single person on earth is the same as another one. There is only one of you. Think about the greatness of our universe, the galaxies, and the stars and planets; everything has been handled with care.

God designed the hours of our days, the days of our weeks, and the months that make up a year. Part of that design was the seventh day, which He blessed and called a special day because by that day He had completed His creation and stopped working. You can find that in Genesis 2:3.

The second thing about which we need to make up our minds: We need to treat that day as sacred. We need to set it apart by dedicating it to God.

Meditate on the following:

- *Is there room for a day of rest in my life right now?*
- *What does it mean for me to dedicate a day to the Lord?*

Journal your thoughts:

5

Our own interests

We should not please ourselves. Instead, we should all please our brothers for their own good, in order to build them up in the faith. For Christ did not please Himself.

Romans 15:2

How wonderful it is to travel through this Bible verse in Isaiah 58 like this. Reading, stopping, thinking, pondering, asking questions, praying, and hearing the Holy Spirit speak deep into our hearts about the issues we face, personally.

I grew up in a Christian family, which meant we went to church on Sundays and prayed for our meals. Although I have no bad memories about the Sundays we spent as a family, there were things unexplainable. We were not allowed to buy ice cream, not even on a blistering hot summer's day when the ice cream vendor came through our street and all the children came running up to his little three-wheel cart.

Of course we asked our parents why we couldn't buy ice cream and I don't remember they ever gave us an answer other than: 'because it is Sunday.' I guess we were not allowed to spend money or to pursue our own interests as mentioned in Isaiah 58;13,

The Lord says, "If you treat the Sabbath as sacred <u>and do not pursue your own interests on that day</u>; if you value my holy day and honor it by not traveling, working, or talking idly on that day..."

This chapter might be a tough one. Most of us probably love to talk about our own interests, and it has been one of our goals in life to pursue those interests. After all, it is our life, our future, and we want to make the best of it.

Well, no reason for panic so far; pursuing our interests is in itself a good thing. God created each human being with interests, desires, dreams, talents, and skills in order to be able to fulfill His divine plan, His purpose for everyone of us. Psalm 139:16 says,

You saw me before I was born. The days allotted to me had all been recorded in your book, before any of them ever began.

It would be disappointing to Him if we didn't go after that purpose, the plan He has for each one of us. He expects us, sooner or later, to discover the greater meaning of life.

In this part of Isaiah 58:13, however, God tells us not to pursue our own interests on that day, the sacred day, the Sabbath. This implies I can pursue my own interests on other days. Doesn't it?

In order to understand God's way of thinking in this part of scripture, we have to let go of our own ideas. I am sure that many people, Christian or not, regard the Sunday as a special day. It is after all part of the weekend in most countries. And if we have the weekend off we just want to do something fun, like going fishing or watching a movie, or going shopping. Something we enjoy doing and something we don't have much time for during the week because we are working (either inside or outside the home) or going to school.

For some people Sundays are a blessing and a good excuse to get away from the house, the homework, or the family, and do something for themselves. Now, why would God tell us *not* to do something for ourselves? That just doesn't make sense, does it? If Saturday or Sunday is a special day to us, why change it? This reflects for most of us the common way of thinking. If, for whatever reason, we regard one day a week as special, we regard it as *our* special day and thus we want to do the things *we* like and love to do.

God's way of thinking, the uncommon way, goes like this: One day a week is special. It is not yours, it is Mine. Pursue Me and not your own interests.

Let's think for a moment about the principle of tithing (giving ten percent of all our income to the Lord). God wants His children to tithe, to give ten percent of all their blessings back to Him, so He can bless the other ninety percent. If we apply that same principle to His holy day, it will work the same way. I am not focusing on percentages and numbers here, but in giving in order to set His blessings in motion. If we give Him one day a week, He will bless the other six. Interesting thought, isn't it? If it works with our money, why wouldn't it work with our time?

Let's go back to our daily lives. Just talk to anyone in the street, the store, or even the church. Doesn't it seem that everyone is busy? Doesn't it seem that everyone needs more time or at least a serious break or time-out? Could it be that we lack time during the week to get everything done because we are trying to keep *all* the days for ourselves, because we refuse (maybe unknowingly) to give God His rightful one day a week? If God urges us not to pursue our own interests on that day, but dedicate it to Him, wouldn't He have something special in mind? Wouldn't He be able to bless the other six days during which we *do* pursue our own interests?

I think we are robbing God from His special day in the same way we would be robbing God if we don't give Him the ten percent of our increase. In Malachi 3:9 God says the people are under a curse because they are robbing Him.

Throughout this book, and hopefully throughout the rest of your life, I want to challenge you. If you are one out of those millions of people who are often busy and hardly ever have enough time to get everything done, start giving His special day back to God! Just try it for a season. You will discover that He starts to bless the other six days in a supernatural way. You will always have enough time.

In the previous chapter I wrote about the two things we need to make up our minds about. The first one: we need a day of rest every seventh day. The second one: we need to treat that day as sacred. If you decided positive on these, you are ready to move on to the next level of commitment. Basically, God is saying that if we do not have a special day, we must announce one and if we have done so, we must not use it for ourselves.

As I said in my statement at the beginning of this book., it is not my intention to give a list of rules and laws to make life miserable. This book is not about do's and don't's. it is about common sense when listening to God. It is about receiving blessings as promised by God.

If you are a person who often complains about being so busy and about lacking time to get everything done, stop complaining. It is not going to help; it will certainly not change anything. Why not try what the Bible prescribes? God's law about Sabbath's rest is not a rule to make our lives more complicated, it is a lovely promise to make it more enjoyable.

In Luke 11:46 Jesus very clearly rebuked the Pharisees about the regulations they wanted the people to obey. He told them,

You put into people's backs loads which are hard to carry, but you yourselves will not stretch out a finger to help them carry those loads.

God is not like that. He does not want to burden us; He wants to guide and help us. I simply want us to look into our own lives and find out what kind of interests we normally pursue during the six days of work or school and maybe as well during the seventh day of the week. Do we pursue our own interests during most of the week? Could we change our attitude on the Sabbath? That is the basic question we have to ask ourselves. What do I do during the week? Am I willing not to do those things during the Sabbath?

Again, this is not about good or bad, right or wrong. This is about common sense, God's common sense. Jesus asked the people if they were allowed to do good on the

Sabbath, to help or harm (Mark 3:4). To 'do' means action. We are not asked to be passive on that day. Resting does not mean to be lazy or sleep. Resting means to rest from our daily routines and work.

Doing good means we can go and visit a friend who is sick or lonely. Doing good means we can go and help cook a meal for an elderly person or take someone, who enjoys birds and flowers, out for a hike in the hills. Doing good means to pursue someone else's interests, not our own. When God states that we should not pursue our own interests on that day, He gives us the opportunity to pursue His interests on that day.

His interest, for example, is in us loving Him by meeting with other believers for celebration, worship, giving, and studying His Word. His interest is in us loving other people. God loves people and only by showing care and love for one another does it show that we belong to Him. Romans 13:10 tells us,

If you love someone, you will never do him wrong,; to love, then, is to obey the whole Law.

Going to the mall and spending money on clothes and accessories is not on God's list of things to do for others. That is pursuing our own interest. Washing our car or painting our house is not on God's list of things we do for others. That is pursuing our own interests.

Do you notice the common sense in this? There is nothing wrong with shopping or washing the car, but it is not what God had in mind for His special day. He wants us to focus on Him and others, which is basically the heart of Christianity and should be the focus of our lives all the time with God's special day, the Sabbath, as highlight, as celebration.

Giving ten percent of our increase to God seems a minor gift when we think about the ninety percent we get to keep for ourselves. After all, everything belongs to God, as we can read in Romans 11:36,

For all things were created by Him, and all things exist through Him and for Him.

We are just using His resources and enjoying His blessings. Giving Him one day and keeping the other six for our interests and work should not be too much to ask either. We would be out of our minds to complain about a deal like that.

Give to God what belongs to Him. The Sabbath is His day; He calls it 'My holy day'. By giving Him the hours on that day, He will multiply them and give them back to us during the other days of the week. We will never ever, run out of time again!

This may sound like a very bold statement, but I am drawing from my own experiences and I am not afraid to proclaim God's way to be the truth. I am so excited about God's way to multiply our time that I have to contain myself not to yell in people's faces when discussing their busy, busy lives. It works, believe it or not.

As a bonus, we will discover that when we give God His holy day, it turns out to be much easier to live for Him the other six days of the week as well. It becomes a lifestyle, not just a weekend thing. We will discover that His way is the best way, the only satisfying way.

Meditate on the following:

- *How do I pursue my own interests?*
- *Could I use more time? If yes, for what reason?*
- *Can I think of something I can do for God on His special day?*

Journal your thoughts:

6

Valuable

Whoever has the Spirit, however, is able to judge the value of everything, but no one is able to judge him.

1 Corinthians 2:15

Are you enjoying this journey through Isaiah 58:13? I sure hope so, let's continue.

The Lord says, "If you treat the Sabbath as sacred and do not pursue your own interests on that day; if you value my holy day and honor it by not traveling, working, or talking idly on that day..."

The Dictionary of Oxford Languages describes 'value' as the regard that something is held to deserve; the importance, worth, or usefulness of something. Value is just how much we think something is worth. In this chapter, we need to ask ourselves: Do I want to honor or validate God's special day?

So far, I have asked us to meditate on announcing a Sabbath and on dedicating it to the Lord. I have asked us to think about pursuing our own interests versus pursuing God's interests. I hope and pray we all have decided positively about this and announced a Sabbath in our lives. If so, we are ready to go on to the next level of commitment to our part of this deal.

God wants us to value His holy day. What exactly is value, I had to ask myself. Do I have things of value? What do I value? Whom do I value? Not so long ago, I had to go to the store to get some new ink cartridges for my printer. While I was trying to find my way between the ridiculous amount of different brand names, shapes, colors, sizes, and prices, I noticed that buying a whole new printer was less expensive than buying a set of new color cartridges.

Best of all, a new printer came with two new cartridges. I hesitated, not because I didn't think this was a good deal or I did not want to buy a new printer, but because I was wondering about the value of an advanced high-tech machine like a printer versus a tiny black box with colors in it. Didn't we learn in school that 'value' is the worth of a thing in money or goods at a certain time? I know that at a certain time, printers were expensive, especially the ones that were able to print a good quality color. Times have changed and so the value changed. Not for the cartridges though, they were always expensive and still are.

The point I want to make is this: The word 'value' did not change, but the things we regard as valuable have changed. In the 21st century we definitely do not put the same value tag on marriage that our grandparents did at the beginning of the previous century. We should not have changed the value, but it happened anyway. The same observation is applicable to family life. Maybe we wish we still had some of the so-called old fashioned family values, but we must face reality here, many of us don't. We allow fighting, discord, divorce, and confusion to enter our homes. We somehow lost values along the way.

Think about sexual relationships and activities. Once valued as precious intimacy and communication between married people and a way to reproduce, nowadays it has been reduced by many to a way of getting what we want or to get even with someone who has hurt us. It is being used as a way to self-medicate our disappointments and pains or as a way to feel loved and accepted by just about anyone. Saddest of all, sex is also being used for marketing purposes and has resulted in sex slavery, pornography, and human trafficking.

What used to be valuable has disappeared from our society or has been degraded at least into something old fashioned and extreme. We acknowledge the existence of certain values or goods, but we don't read the price tags anymore. Therefore, we have not decided if we are willing to pay the price.

Take marriage again, for example. We still acknowledge the institution of marriage; people get married every day. A lot of people, however, have no idea what the value tag really is. We don't know if we are able and willing to pay the price. We are greedy. We want to have it, we want the status that comes with it, and we want it now.

Once we have obtained what we wanted (a certain person and position in life) we discover that we cannot afford it. We need to sacrifice to be able to pay the price and sacrifice is not a very popular word nowadays. We want everything to come easy, to be fun, and to give us a happy feeling. But we forget that there is a price to pay.

So, God wants us to value His holy day. Just having that day is not enough, as being married is not enough for a good relationship. We have to value it. Just trying to keep the day for Him is not enough. He wants us to value it, to think highly of it. Reading through this book you might think, 'okay, it seems I need a special day dedicated to the Lord. Whatever. I'll set one up and get it over with. Maybe I will get something out of this after all.'

That is not the way God has in mind. He wants us to value that day. Just keeping the Sabbath holy does not tell anything about our attitude. Just being married to someone doesn't tell anything about the way that relationship is going. Just giving an offering doesn't tell anything about our true generosity in daily life.

A lot of Christians keep laws, regulations, and practice religious habits without knowing why. When asked, they simply reply: 'My parents did it, everyone in my church does it, I don't know, I never gave it a thought,' etc. etc. So God did not add this note as a less important remark. No, He put emphasis on the point He wants to make.

God does not want anyone just to do as He says with a 'whatever' attitude. He very clearly specifies His desires and requests. He wants us to think about our actions and attitudes. It may be helpful to think about the principle of tithing and giving again. God doesn't just tell us to give. He prefers it a certain way. In 2 Corinthians 9:7 (KJV), we can read that…

God loves a cheerful giver.

He does not want us to give our tithes and offerings to Him out of duty or obligation or, worse, because everyone does it. He wants us to give Him something because we love Him, because we appreciate Him, because we are thankful to Him. He wants us to give happily. That is just the way He likes it.

I feel free to apply the same principle to the Sabbath. He wants us to value that day. He wants us to be serious about it. He doesn't want us to take it lightly. If you feel you would like to know more about the Sabbath, about the Jewish customs on that day, about historical values or theological views, please check the internet or your library. You probably need a lifetime to read everything that has ever been written about it.

People have debated the purpose of the Sabbath, argued about the value in our modern day, and questioned the true meaning. It is okay to study this subject further, to meditate and pray on it, as long as you keep the Bible as your reference guide. Being serious about God's holy day for starters is a way of valuing it.

Meditate on the following:

- *What do I regard as valuable in my life?*
- *Do I do things just because everyone is doing it?*

Journal your thoughts:

7

Honor

And My father will honor anyone who serves me

John 12:26b

In Webster's Dictionary, the verb 'to value' is explained as: to think highly of. God wants us to think highly of His holy day. In Isaiah 58:13 God further adds: 'And honor it.'

The Lord says, "If you treat the Sabbath as sacred and do not pursue your own interests on that day; if you value my holy day and honor it by not traveling, working, or talking idly on that day..."

To honor something or someone can be done in many ways. In the next chapter, we will read how God has that in mind on this particular subject. For now, let us think about honor and it's different meanings. According to Webster's, to honor is:

* To respect greatly; regard highly; esteem

- To show great respect or high regard for; treat with deference and courtesy
- To worship
- To confer and honor on; exalt; ennoble
- To accept and pay when due

Honor is a word and attitude that seems to be slowly disappearing from our culture. Honoring people has been replaced with blaming, shaming, and even canceling people, which is quite tragic if you ask me. Honoring parents, teachers, leaders, even God, is not a popular topic. Instead, we see indifference and selfishness. A popular slogan in modern-day society is: 'it is my life and I do what I want.' In other words, I am not going to listen to anyone. Mind your own business. I'll find my way. You will, indeed.

In chapter three, I described our society as one that is proud of her independence and self-help structure. We can figure it all out if given enough time and money. I think that a result of living in this society is the fact that we find it very difficult to accept correction and guidance. After all, we want to find out ourselves. We do not like to be taken by the hand and guided into a different direction. We do not want to go off our familiar track. What if we get lost? What if we meet strangers?

We are self-supporting, and in case we really need some help in certain troubled areas of our lives, we can always seek professional help. Nowadays, there seems to be a therapist for just about everything. But then again, we switch doctors and therapists as if they were a pair of jeans. If we don't like the direction they are sending us in, we leave. We keep looking for someone who or something that will tell us what we want to hear. People go from yoga to Pilates, from massage therapy to psychics, even from church to church, searching for anything or anyone who will agree with the way they already think.

Yes, we want our help to come from a direction that we are comfortable with, something we can feel at peace with. This attitude has already been foreseen in God's Word. In 2 Timothy 4:3 we can read the following warning:

The time will come when people will not listen to sound doctrine, but will follow their own desires and will collect for themselves more and more teachers who will tell them what they are itching to hear.

I think we should ask ourselves if we only honor the people and methods that somehow appeal to us. Are we able to honor God's laws that correct us and sometimes guide us into an opposite direction?

God is very specific on how to honor the Sabbath, His way. We don't have to figure out how and we certainly don't have to make 'rules'. He has it all written down for us, very plain, very simple. Maybe you are one of many people who regard the Ten Commandments as old fashioned and no longer applicable today. The fourth commandment about honoring the Sabbath is no longer relevant for us today. Or is it? Let's not forget that the Sabbath is mentioned throughout the Bible, not just in the Law. There is a progressive revelation about the Sabbath throughout the scriptures. Let's take a look.

The Sabbath in the Torah

Although the term 'sabbath' is not mentioned in Genesis, we know from the story of creation that God blessed the seventh day of the week. We can read that in Genesis 2:3 (NLT),

And God blessed the seventh day and declared it holy, because it was the day when he rested from all his work of creation.

Later on, throughout the book of Exodus, we can see how this declaration of a holy day became engraved as law, as part of a perpetual covenant between God and the Jewish people. In Exodus 31:16-17 we can read the following:

Therefore the children of Israel shall keep the Sabbath, to observe the Sabbath throughout their generations as a perpetual covenant. It is a sign between Me and the children of Israel forever; for in six days the Lord made

the heavens and the earth, and on the seventh day He rested and was refreshed.

The day is meant for us to rest and be refreshed so we can fully embrace the week ahead!

The Sabbath in the book of Psalms

Psalm 92 is a song to be sung on the Sabbath day. It says that it is good to praise the Lord and make music to His name, proclaiming His love in the morning and His faithfulness at night. The Sabbath is a joyful day!

The Sabbath in the prophetic books

The base scripture I have used for this book is Isaiah 58:13-14. However, Isaiah was not the only prophet receiving words from the Lord about the Sabbath. Other prophets make mention of the Sabbath as well, such as Jeremiah, Ezekiel, Hosea, and Amos. Jeremiah repeatedly reminded the people to take their God-given rest and to not carry heavy loads. The instructions he received came from the Lord, as we can read in Jeremiah 17:21-22 for example,

Tell them that if they love their lives, they must not carry any load on the Sabbath; they must not carry anything in through the gates of Jerusalem or carry anything out of their houses on the Sabbath. They must not work on the

Sabbath; they must observe it as a sacred day, as I commanded their ancestors.

It has never been God's plan to make the lives of His beloved people, and us for that matter, miserable and complicated. He wants the best for all His children! You probably heard that many times before and may even regard that as a cliché. But think about the loads many people are carrying, emotional and spiritual loads. Some people get overloaded and eventually collapse. The Sabbath could prevent this way of stressful living!

The Sabbath in the Gospels

Jesus spoke about the Sabbath on several occasions, especially to correct the religious leaders who accused Him and His disciples of healing people on the Sabbath and walking through the fields, picking grain. His conclusion (Mark 3:27-28) concerning the Sabbath debate was as follows:

And Jesus concluded, "The Sabbath was made for the good of human beings; they were not made for the Sabbath. So the Son of Man is Lord even of the Sabbath."

The Sabbath was made for our own good!

The Sabbath in the Epistles

Last, but not least, the Sabbath is mentioned in the book of Acts and in the Epistles. The apostle Paul finally distanced himself from his legalistic point of view and declared:

So let no one make rules about what you eat or drink or about holy days or the New Moon Festival or the Sabbath. All such things are only a shadow of things in the future; the reality is Christ (Colossians 2:16-17).

There is no punishment for not keeping the Sabbath, for our reality is Christ. However, we will miss out on special blessings when we ignore the principle of taking a day of rest after every six days of work.

Think for a moment about what has been written in John 10:10, where Jesus talks about His purpose here on earth.

I have come in order that you might have life-life in all its fullness.

A life in all its fullness, do we ever really think about that? Do we live this life He came to give us? I wrote about that extensively in my book 'Grace of Giving.' This wonderful promise is being preceded by a warning, stated in the first part of that same scripture.

The thief comes only in order to steal, kill and destroy.

Yes, God wants the best for us and yes, there is also someone out there to destroy our joy, our peace, and our lives. I think it is very important, while thinking about honoring the Sabbath, that we keep John 10:10 in mind.

It is not God's intention to make our lives difficult. He wants us to fully enjoy and live our lives. He wants to help us by setting up guidelines and healthy boundaries. It is up to us to choose to follow them.

Do we want to live by His guidance or don't we? Do we want the quality of our lives to be improved or don't we? In case of the Sabbath, do we want our time to be supernaturally blessed or don't we ?

For centuries, people have been discussing God's laws, commandments, regulations, and guidelines. Somehow, God's orders were altered, changed, misunderstood, or simply ignored. Many people have been trying to be better people by telling others what to do and what not to do. Somehow, I think we have often been missing the point.

God's laws are not about being a better person than the other. God's laws are not about gaining favor with some folks around us or even with God Himself. He has set up His rules for the lives of His children, and in doing so He gave us a way of expressing our love for Him. In 1 John 5:3 it says,

Four our love for God meant that we obey His commands. And His commands are not too hard for us.

Yes, we can express our love for God by obeying Him! His commands are about blessings; they are about a full life. In Isaiah 48:18 God says:

If only you had listened to My commands! Then blessings would have flowed for you like a stream that never goes dry.

His commands are about a way of life that God had it in mind when He created us.

Meditate on the following:

- *Do I honor God and His Word? If yes, how?*
- *What stops me from taking a day of rest every week?*
- *Am I willing to re-think a day of rest?*

Journal your thoughts:

8

Daily application

Your instructions give me pleasure; they are my advisers.

Psalm 119:24

In Isaiah 58:13, God gives us three clues on how to honor His holy day. I want us to think about all three of them.

The Lord says, "If you treat the Sabbath as sacred and do not pursue your own interests on that day; if you value my holy day and honor it <u>by not traveling, working, or talking idly on that day...</u>"

Please, don't get discouraged and say: 'I can never live up to that' or 'I don't really see how that can possibly be practical in my life.' Remember, these guidelines are given to make our lives better. Let's see how to apply them to our daily lives.

Traveling

We can honor God's day by not traveling. That is a statement that almost seems weird in our modern-day society. If we can't travel, we can't go anywhere, and what good will it do to stay in the house for twenty-four hours? Slumping on the couch and watching television is not going to make our lives better, is it?

Within Jewish orthodox circles many rules have been made regarding the Sabbath. Some of them based on the scriptures, others not. Rules include: no work is to be done which includes tasks such as cooking and driving and not lighting candles after sunset on Friday. There are even rules about the amount of steps one can take on a Sabbath.

Remember what we read in Colossians 2:16,

So let no one make rules about what you eat or drink or about holy days or the New Moon Festival or the Sabbath.

No one makes the rules, God does. This book is not about rules, it is about guidelines and choices.

It is interesting what Isaiah 58:13 in the New King James version says:

If you turn away your foot from the Sabbath, From doing your pleasure on My holy day, And call the Sabbath a delight, The holy day of the Lord honorable, And shall honor Him, not doing your own ways, Nor finding your own pleasure, Nor speaking your own words…

'Not doing you own ways' has been translated as 'not traveling' in the Good News Translation. That makes sense, doesn't it? Traveling is doing our own thing, not being concerned about others. I will not give a definition on traveling versus moving. I am not going to discuss whether going to the beach is traveling, whether driving our car to church is traveling, or whether flying to a three-day conference in Dallas, for example, is traveling.

I simply want us to go back to chapter three and think. I hope you have made up your mind about no longer pursuing your own interests on the Sabbath. I hope you came up with God's interests. If you already have a vision on how that will change the holy day, the proposal not to travel, not to do your own thing, will be an easy one. We have to ask ourself this question the moment we want to leave the house to go somewhere: 'Do I pursue God's interest with this?'

It doesn't really matter if we are about to get in the car and drive to the mall, to the beach, to the theater, to a friend, or to church. Just take a moment and think; what is the reason for my traveling? Is it for God, someone else, or myself?

If for some reason we have been out of town on business, vacation, or on a family visit and we are thinking about driving or flying back on our day of rest, take a minute and think. Is there a possibility to go back a day earlier or a day later maybe? We may find that we have traveled many times without thinking about possible alternatives.

We should no longer ask ourselves if it is allowed to do certain things on the Sabbath, like the Pharisees did. The true question we should ask ourselves from now on would be: 'What am I pursuing? My own interests or God's interests? In this case, take the time to find out if there is a way to honor God's day by rearranging your (!) travel schedule.

Working

We can honor God's day by not working.

I am not going to discuss the ethics of working. This book is about trying to change the way we probably always lived. Working is simply something we do to earn a living or to support a household. When God says: 'Do not work', He means 'do not work-not for money and not to pursue our own interests. The King James version calls it 'nor finding thine own pleasure.'

Again, we should ask ourselves the following question: 'What am I pursuing? My own interests or God's interests? If we are about to get something done on the holy day, we can ask ourself if we do pursue God's interest with this. Just wait a minute and think. If we have a paid job that requires us to work without a regular day off, we could ask yourself if it is really the dream job we wanted; maybe it wouldn't hurt to apply for something else or maybe we could ask our boss to be off on the holy day. Again, we may find that we work many times without questioning ourselves about the job.

Talking idly

We can honor God's day by not talking idly.

I am not sure if this is a word that is still being used. Personally, I had to look it up in the dictionary. God does not want us to talk idly on His day. A dictionary will give us many synonyms, but it all comes down to this: Do not talk worthless, useless, vain, futile, pointless or ineffective. We might have a tendency to talk 'bull' with our friends in school, with our co-workers, with our buddies in the gym, or with whomever and wherever. I don't think there is anything wrong with joking around. I don't think it is a sin to talk about nothing, so to say. In light of the Sabbath however, God makes a clear and simple statement: 'You can honor My day by not talking idly.'

We can ask ourselves this simple question when we are about to open our mouth on His day: 'What I am about to say, will it build me and the other person up? Not talking idly might be the most difficult of the three, but it will be the most rewarding as well. Other people will notice the difference in our attitude, they will truly appreciate our efforts, and we will meet more smiles and make more people happy than we can ever think of.

Meditate on the following:

- *Do I want my life to be change? If so, in what areas?*
- *Not traveling, working, and talking idly-what would be the most difficult for me and why?*
- *Do I think before I talk?*

Journal your thoughts:

Pray aloud:

Dear Father in Heaven, thank You for giving me seven days a week to enjoy my life. I want to give to You what belongs to You. Thank You for giving me work, hobbies, and interests, for giving me things to do. Please help me to pursue Your interests, not out of obligation, but out of love. Holy Spirit, help me to value and understand the Word every time I read it or hear it. Please help me to change my mind about always being so busy.

Dear God, I want to dedicate my life to You with Your special day as the highlight of every week. Thank you for honoring me. You gave Your first and only Son to save my life from sins and destruction. What an awesome offer! I want to honor You. Thank You for guiding me into a better life with more time, more joy, and more fulfillment. I ask You, Holy Spirit, to help me to rearrange my schedule according to the Father's plan. In the name of Jesus, I pray this. Amen.

Part II

Then you will find the joy that comes from serving me. I will make you honored all over the world, and you will enjoy the land I gave to your ancestor, Jacob. I, the Lord, have spoken.

Isaiah 58:14

9

Open mind

If your law had not been the source of my joy, I would have died from my sufferings.

Psalm 119:92

Now we are getting to the easy part of this book, the blessing! After all that is God's part of the deal. I love it when we read 'then' in the Bible, because it is always followed by a blessing. Isaiah 58:14 says,

<u>*Then you will find the joy*</u> *that comes from serving me. I will make you honored all over the world, and you will enjoy the land I gave to your ancestor, Jacob. I, the Lord, have spoken.*

Wouldn't it be wonderful if we could see and experience God's commandments as loving guidelines from a parent to a dear child? Some people find it difficult to look at His commandments that way, because their parents or pastor or youth leader used to scare them with such rules. Some people may be blind to the heart of God's commandments because all they can see is the punishment that may come when disobeying. I urge you to read Psalm 119 from a translation that speaks to you. The writer is truly excited about God's Law, but that didn't come to him without effort. He prays for understanding in verse 33,

Teach me, Lord, the meaning of Your laws.

I believe a lot of people find it hard to look at commandments that way because they don't look at it with the help of the Holy Spirit.

In chapter three, I compared our attitudes towards God's Word with the attitudes we use when handling an assembly manual. We get irritated before we even start reading. There are thoughts, pre-conceived ideas, in our minds that tell us that what we are about to read will be hard and difficult to understand. In other words, our inner being fights before even attacked. This is simply another thing that God did foresee. That is why He gave us His Holy Spirit, who is also called the Helper.

In 2 Corinthians 3:6 (NIV), we can see how the Spirit is able to bring life to the scriptures.

He has made us competent as ministers of a new covenant-not of the letter but of the Spirit; for the letter kills, but the Spirit gives life.

Most of us probably remember fighting some of our parent's rules, thinking they were way old fashioned and not applicable in the century we lived in. We also know that most of their rules were there to protect us and give us a fair chance in life. Deep in our hearts, we know most of their rules were even there because they loved us and they did not want any harm to come to us.

In the same way, I truly believe our lives could be easier and more relaxed when we would live out God's commandments, for they are good in itself! Reading the commandments with the help of the Holy Spirit residing in us, changes everything. They rather sound like sincere advice then law enforcement regulations, advice that will bring success and blessings when applied. When we allow ourselves to read God's Word with an open mind, without going on the offensive before He even has finished His first line, and without pre-conceived ideas, we will discover that God is sincere in guiding us. He does not want us to get lost somewhere down the road of our life's journey.

I cannot put enough emphasis on the fact that this book is not about salvation, forgiveness, getting to heaven, or receiving eternal life. This is not about being a better person than the one next to you. Nobody can earn his or her way into heaven by pleasing God. We will always fall short. Only God's grace and our faith can accomplish that. This book is about a better life while here on earth, a life in all its fullness. Remember John 10:10? A life God had in mind when He created us in His image.

This book is about how God, in the Old Testament, describes the way He wants us to live and about how Jesus, in the New Testament, explains us how to do that. In Matthew 12:7 Jesus discusses the Sabbath with a group of religious folks. He takes them back to the Old Testament where it says,

It is kindness that I want, not animal sacrifices.

This book is not about sacrifices, about do's and don't's that will make our life complicated and maybe even miserable. This book is about love and kindness. Love, first of all toward the God who made us, and second, to the people around us. Jesus is the ultimate example on how to love the way God wants it. In Matthew 5;17 (NIV) He says:

Do not think that I have come to abolish the Law or the Prophets; I have not come to abolish them but to fulfill them.

We can discuss and debate the Ten Commandments, and in this case, the keeping of the Sabbath, as long as we want, but when we look at the Law the way Jesus did, it suddenly makes sense. He came to fulfill it. We can do so as well.

Being a Christian simply means being Christlike. Jesus is the example of a Christian life. Simply imitating Jesus without accepting His grace would lead us nowhere. Trying to obey His teachings without accepting the forgiveness of our sins would only lead to frustration. The Bible speaks very clearly about the position we all have in Christ, for example in Acts 15:11,

We believe and are saved by the grace of the Lord Jesus.

We need His grace. With our sinful nature, we could never, ever even come close to fulfilling the Law the way Jesus did. That is why Jesus shared our sin in order that we could share in His righteousness. There is an absolutely powerful scripture about that concept in 2 Corinthians 5:21,

Christ was without sin, but for our sake God made Him share our sin in order that in union with Him we might share the righteousness of God.

Hallelujah! Once we have accepted God's grace, it turns out to be an honor to fulfill the Law in love, the way Jesus did. We will start pleasing God because we are thankful and not because we are trying to be in a better position with Him. We will show our love to God, not by reading the letter, but by simply obeying it in life and love. Instead of going around telling people what they can and cannot do, we can do acts of love and kindness as described in chapter five and fulfill what God has in mind. He promises in Deuteronomy 7:9 to,

Show His constant love to a thousand generations of those who love Him and obey His commandments.

Meditate on the following:

- *How do I experience the help of the Holy Spirit in Bible reading?*
- *Fulfilling the Law... what comes to mind?*

Journal your thoughts:

10

Finding joy

Your commandments are my eternal possession; they are the joy of my heart.

Psalm 119:111

Much of scripture can be divided into two parts, basically the same way as this book, an obedience part and a blessings part. It is amazing how many scriptures we can find where God tells us to do something and promises blessings in return when we follow His instructions.

So, let us get to God's part as we can read it in Isaiah 58:14, the blessing. We all want to be blessed, right?

<u>*Then you will find the joy*</u> *that comes from serving me. I will make you honored all over the world, and you will enjoy the land I gave to your ancestor, Jacob. I, the Lord, have spoken.*

Isaiah 58:14 starts with *'Then you will find the joy...'* God promises us joy! He promises a special kind of joy, as we will discover in the next chapter. For now, I want

us to think about joy. Do you agree with me that, in general, it seems joy has disappeared from society? Let's face the facts here, so many people struggle with anxiety, worries, pain, mental illnesses and disorders, depression, and even suicidal thoughts. It is obvious that there is a thief at work who wants to steal and kill our joy. The other side of the coin is that God wants to give it to us, in abundance. Joy is fruit of the Holy Spirit.

The Bible talks about different kinds of joy that Christians can experience. Here are some of them:

- **The joy of salvation**

In Psalm 51:12 (NKJV), we can read about our greatest joy, the joy of salvation. Whether we have a sense of humor or not, whether we are an introvert or extrovert, whether we are rather pessimistic or not, we can all experience the joy of salvation by simply asking for it as the psalmist did.

Restore to me the joy of Your salvation, And uphold me by Your generous Spirit.

Maybe you have asked the Lord, but see no joy in your life. The Bible says the joy of our salvation can be restored. It is a gift from God Himself, to us; it is a fruit of the Holy Spirit who dwells in us after we are born again, and it just needs to be protected, cultivated, and watered in order to make it grow.

- **The joy of the Lord**

In Nehemiah 8:10 (NIV) the prophet declares,

The joy of the Lord is your strength.

What a powerful statement. Nehemiah says this to the people, because they had been weeping while listening to the Law being read. Do not be sad, be joyful, it is your strength. The Bible talks here about a joy that is not human; it is a divine kind of happiness and it will strengthen us.

- **The joy of my heart**

Are you ready for this one? Psalm 119:111 speaks about the joy of our heart. The psalmist speaks about his love for God's law:

Your commandments are my eternal possession; they are the joy of my heart.

Think about it, just studying this book and the commandments in general should fill us with joy! God's guidance should bring us joy. Not just a smile on our faces, but true joy in our hearts.

- **Everlasting joy**

Isaiah 51:11 (NIV) talks about everlasting joy that will crown the heads of the people who will return to Zion.

He talks about a joy that will never stop. A joy that will last forever.

- **The joy of serving God**

In the next chapter we will look into this special kind of joy.

Now, of course there is lot more to be said about joy as mentioned in the Bible. The book of Philippians, for example, is nicknamed the book of joy because it speaks so much about this particular topic. Listen to Paul's words in Philippians 4:4 for example:

May you always be joyful in your union with the Lord. I say it again: rejoice!

What a wonderful scripture. Personally I love the word joy. It means so much more to me than happiness. We can be happy because someone has been kind to us, because the sun is shining, or because we have received a present. Happiness is the result of happenings. Happiness is the result of certain positive circumstances or benevolent actions done to or for us. How often do we say: 'Yes, that will make me happy.' Something needs to be done to produce that feeling.

Joy is something we have, regardless of the circumstances. Happiness is temporarily, joy is eternal. Happiness is the result of something happening to us. Joy is a possession; it doesn't come and go like happiness or even pleasure or enjoyment. Let's say joy is divine happiness. Joy is part of God's divine character. He likes to share it with us through His Holy Spirit. In Galatians 5:22 we can learn what God's character is all about.

But the Spirit produces love, joy, peace, patience, kindness, goodness, faithfulness, humility, and self-control.

Joy is a product of God's character in us. We have it even if we don't feel happy. Happiness goes up and down with our circumstances; joy is permanent. It is a divine gift from God to us. Joy is a product of the Holy Spirit and does not depend on what other people do for us. It is something on the inside that is always there and it is the result of what Jesus did for us. That is why joy is so much better than just mere happiness; it lasts. Do you know anyone who always seems at peace and joyful, even if things go wrong? Do you wish you could have more joy and be less anxious?

The Bible promises us joy if we treat the Sabbath as sacred. It is no question whether we will have it or not. Isaiah 58:14 says: 'Then you will find the joy…' I love that word 'then', it means after that, thus, accordingly, consequently. You will find it if you look for it. You will find it if you try. Finding something only occurs when we have been looking for it.

You may be a Christian and so the Holy Spirit lives inside of you, but yet you are not joyful. Is it possible that the Holy Spirit forgot to produce joy in your life? No! Joy will be there when the Spirit is present. That is a promise according to Galatians 5:22. Joy is a fruit produced by the Spirit in the life of every believer. Sometimes we simply have to look for it and stir it up.

Let's say we have a garage, basement, or attic full of stuff that we don't even remember storing there. We do not know what we actually possess, just because we hardly ever go through the pile. We forgot! Sometimes that happens with the gifts God gave us. We pray, we ask, we whine, we receive, and we put it in storage. It is time to organize our stuff. We may find long forgotten treasures deep down in our heart, where God has placed it to begin with. Life has a tendency to pile her troubles on our treasures, so we have to be careful.

Joy is something to be treasured. The specific joy that the Lord promises us here, will be found only if… And for the 'if' we have to go back to Isaiah 58:13 again and read the first eight chapters of this book. Obedience and blessing-the two are tied together the way seed and harvest are tied together. We cannot have one without the other. Aren't you excited about teaming up with God? If we do our part, He will do His part.

Meditate on the following:

- *How do I see the Ten Commandments?*
- *Do I accept guidance and correction in my life? If yes, from whom?*
- *What gives me happiness? What takes away my happiness?*

Journal your thoughts:

11

Serving the Lord

Remember that the Lord will give you as a reward what He has kept for his people. For Christ is the real Master you serve.

Colossians 3:24

In Isaiah 58:14 God promises that we will find the joy that comes from serving Him if we treat the Sabbath as sacred.

Then you will find the joy <u>that comes from serving me</u>. I will make you honored all over the world, and you will enjoy the land I gave to your ancestor, Jacob. I, the Lord, have spoken.

Serving God is a term commonly used within Christian circles. By that we mean that we wait on Him, we serve Him, in other words we do what He asks us to do. In our daily world serving and waiting are terms reserved for the work certain people do in restaurants. Servers or waitresses, for that matter, are occupations. People do it because they get paid for it.

Do we know what it means to serve the Lord? When talking about someone who serves the Lord, do we think about a pastor in a big church, a volunteer who works with the poor and homeless, an evangelist who works in third-world countries, or a teenager who gave up a year of his/her life to go abroad to Bible school? What does it mean to serve the Lord, and if we do serve Him, is it possible to find joy in that?

How do we serve the Lord in our daily lives? How do we put that into practice? Let's look into some plain, simple, and Biblical ways to serve God in our churches and in our daily lives. We can start putting them into practice today.

First of all, we need to keep in mind that we are not asked to serve God because He needs anything from us. In Acts 17:25 we can find a powerful statement:

Nor does He [God] *need anything that we can supply by working for Him, since it is He Himself who gives life and breath and everything else to everyone.*

God does not need our service, but He wants us to serve Him by serving others. That is what He loves. We can find ways to serve the Lord throughout the whole Bible. In Deuteronomy 10:12-22, we are given an account of serving God in different ways. Verse 12b says,

Love Him, serve Him with all your heart, and obey all His laws.

Loving, serving, and obeying cannot be separated.

I want to put it this way: out of love for God we will serve others and in doing so we will obey Him.

In Deuteronomy 10:12 we will find that God blends service to Him with service to other people. We simply cannot love God and not love our neighbor. We cannot truly love our neighbor without loving God. We can try, but we will find it very hard at times. Serving God has always two sides to it: Him and others. We can read this in Matthew 22:37-40 where Jesus answers one of the Pharisees who came to Him with a question about the greatest commandment in the Law. His answer was as follows:

'Love the Lord your God with all your heart, with all your soul, and with all your mind.' This is the greatest and the most important commandment. The second most important commandment is like it: 'Love your neighbor as you love yourself.' The whole Law of Moses and the teachings of the prophets depend on these two commandments.

When reading Jesus' words, it becomes clear why we cannot obey God without love. To love is to obey. Just reading the commandments and keeping the letter is not what Jesus asks. He wants us to fulfill the commandments in love. The apostle Paul truly understood this lesson as we can read in Romans 13:8-10 (NIV), emphasis mine:

Let no debt remain outstanding, except the continuing debt to love one another, <u>for whoever loves others has fulfilled the law.</u> The commandments, "You shall not commit adultery," "You shall not murder," "You shall not steal," "You shall not covet," and whatever other command there may be, are summed up in this one command: "Love your neighbor as yourself." Love does no harm to a neighbor. <u>Therefore love is the fulfillment of the law</u>.

When we say we cannot fulfill the Law, we are basically saying we are unable to love. Think about that!

Anyway, let's continue in Deuteronomy chapter 10, we come to verse 19 where God says:

So then, show love for those foreigners, because you were once foreigners in Egypt.

God speaks about showing love to foreigners. And yes, He obviously addresses the Israelites here, but as we read these words today He addresses you and me as well. Jesus summarized the old teachings in Matthew 7:12 and made them applicable for today,

Do for others what you want them to do for you: this is the meaning of the Law of Moses and of the teachings of the prophets.

So, let's ask ourselves, do we have a new person in our class? Let's make up our minds to treat him or her nicely and make him or her feel welcome, for we were once newcomers ourselves. Is there a new colleague at work? Let's help him to find his way, introduce ourselves, and make him feel comfortable in the new workplace, for we stepped into that office or factory a first time as well. Have new people, no matter where they are coming from, moved into our neighborhood? Let's welcome them, shake their hand, bake a pie and take it over to their house, for many of us were once strangers in town as well.

Maybe we notice a first time visitor in our church. Let's walk up to that person and welcome him or her. When we first became believers my husband and I visited different churches in America before we started to attend the Solid Rock Christian Center in Ventura, CA. We noticed that the friendly treatment of first time visitors was much better in traditional churches than in some evangelical or non-denominational churches. Greeters smothered us with hugs and kisses. Well, it could be that the traditional churches were more anxious to get new members, but still, shouldn't we all work hard to make strangers feel at home?

Do you see how easily we can translate these principles of serving into our daily routines and lives? In the same chapter, Deuteronomy 10, God speaks about reverence and faithfulness to Him. Verse 20,

Have reverence for the Lord your God and worship only Him. Be faithful to Him and make your promises in His name alone.

God reminds us to be as serious about Him as He is about us. We should ask ourselves if we worship anyone other than Him. Maybe it is our partner, a movie idol, a favorite baseball player. Maybe it is our job or our money that is getting more attention and time than God. you can find more about this in my book 'True Worshipers'. We should ask ourselves if we are faithful to God. Did we promise Him to attend church regularly, to pray every day, or to study a particular part of scripture every day? Are we faithful to our promises? If it is hard to keep all our promises to God, we should start with one promise and keep it until it becomes part of our daily lives, like getting dressed, eating, and drinking.

Romans 12 is a chapter in the New Testament describing a life in God's service. It offers a lot of possibilities to serve God in spiritual as well as practical ways. Verse 11 and 12 for example:

- *Work hard and do not be lazy*
- *Serve the Lord with a heart full of devotion*

- *Let your hope keep you joyful*
- *Be patient in your troubles, and*
- *Pray at all times*
- *Share your belongings with your needy fellow Christians, and*
- *Open your homes to strangers.*

Again, God blends service to Himself with service to others. Praying without helping others is not what He has in mind neither is helping others without praying. We may pray, Lord help my friend with his homework. I know he is struggling. We may pray and pray. Don't you think God wants us to help that person? So many of our prayers are questions. Lord, will You do this and that? Many times the solution, the answer, is in our own hands. We just have to do what we have to do: serve others. Go and help that friend and pray for guidance.

Maybe a friend or neighbor needs a pick-up truck to move some items. Maybe we can lend him ours or we could do the job with him. Maybe someone is struggling to get the computer or smartphone working properly. We could offer help and our computer skills for an afternoon. Are some folks from out of town visiting church? Maybe they can stay at our place. Just try to put into practice what the Bible says. Reading and living God's Word are totally different things. Work and pray, pray and work!

Being joyful and being patient are ways of serving the Lord as well. If others can see that we are joyful under circumstances that require super strength and courage, they might see Jesus in us. If others can see we are patient under circumstances that require self-discipline and special kindness, they might recognize Christ in us and that brings glory to God.

We can also serve God by serving His church. He loves it when we get involved the way He has in mind. 1 Corinthians 12:5 explains:

There are different ways of serving, but the same Lord is served.

The Bible shows us in 1 Corinthians 12 how we can serve God and each other in our churches. Verse 6 says,

There are different abilities to perform service, but the same God gives ability to everyone for their particular service.

1 Corinthians 12:8-10 provides a list of nine gifts as given by the Holy Spirit to Christians. They are needed for building up the church. God's church (whether local or universal) is a living organism. It moves, it grows, and it changes. The Bible uses the metaphor of a human body with all its different parts. As humans we don't merely exist, we live. We take care of our body, we feed it well, we exercise if we want to keep it in shape, we grow and

change. The church needs the same kind of attention in order to grow and become beautiful and gracious. By serving God and one another we get equipped to go out and serve all people!

I realize this chapter gives only a short list of all the ways we can serve the Lord. Basically, serving the Lord has three aspects to it:

1. Serving God
2. Serving others
3. Serving the church

God promises us joy when we serve Him. By now, we have seen that joy will not come when we do things out of duty, fear, or peer pressure. Joy from serving comes when we do it out of love. God has set it up that way; if we obey Him because we love Him, He will reward us. We will just want to do more and more for Him. Serving will become a desire of our hearts.

Treating the Sabbath as sacred will become a desire of our hearts as well and it will bring joy, unspeakable joy. When we do something for God out of love He will reward us with joy, and because we find so much joy in doing that for Him, we want to do more for Him. In other words, we will discover that we just love serving Him!

Meditate on the following:

- *What does it mean to me when someone serves the Lord?*
- *Who or what do I serve on a daily basis and how?*
- *What promise do I want to make to God and what do I need to do to keep that promise?*

Journal your thoughts:

12

All over the world

And My Father will honor anyone who serves Me

John 12:26b

The promised blessing in Isaiah 58:14 has a double function. It contains personal blessings as well as a corporate blessing.

Then you will find the joy that comes from serving me. I will make you honored all over the world, and you will enjoy the land I gave to your ancestor, Jacob. I, the Lord, have spoken.

In the previous chapters, the first personal blessing has been discussed, namely the joy that comes from serving God. In the next chapter, the second personal blessing will be discussed, namely: we will enjoy the land God gave to our ancestor Jacob. Both blessings deal with joy. God promises joy to those who treat the Sabbath as sacred.

God also promises honor. 'I will make you honored all over the world' sounds more like a blessing for a whole nation or a group of people than for an individual, although it could be both of course. It has a prophetic ring to it. I would like to call that the corporate blessing.

As a European who has resided in the USA, I have met quite a few Americans who suspected that people from other countries thought negatively about the USA because of social and political scandals. Many times people have asked us: 'What do you Europeans think about us? Do people like us over there?' Maybe you have never asked a foreigner that question, but I noticed that in general, people do really care what others think and say about them as a nation. No matter where we live, we want people to speak well about our country.

That is why it is so interesting to read what God promises the people who honor the Sabbath day: I will make you honored all over the world.' That is an awesome promise, isn't it? Although He made that promise to the ancient Israelites and not to us, I believe it is certainly a promise *for* us. I want us to think of this as a promise that God made to all future believers. It is a promise He makes today to those who treat the Sabbath as sacred.

I remember when America was honored all over the world. As a child, I heard the heroic stories about World War II, about our liberators, about people offering their lives for our freedom. I don't know whether America has changed her military liberation policies, but somehow she is no longer honored all over the world. Is it possible that the worldwide honoring has disappeared because of the lack of Sabbath keeping? I am just thinking out loud and I hope you get the point. I truly believe it can be turned around again!

After promising us joy, God almost casually adds the next promise in Isaiah 58:14, the corporate blessing:

I will make you honored all over the world.

This chapter has probably been the most difficult one to write. I had so many questions. I asked God, for example, whom He had in mind, besides the Israelites, when He said 'I will make you honored all over the world.' I also asked Him what that would look like. When we read that scripture as an individual, it is hard to imagine how God is going to honor us all over the world.

If, however, we read it for the country we live in, we might wonder if He wants to make the whole nation honored all over the world. Maybe just all the Christians or certain churches? How is honoring going to take place on a worldwide scale? I understood that the 'how' is not up to us, that is up to Him. The 'who' will be solved when the honoring starts to happen. The first scripture that came to my mind was Luke 6:38b,

The measure you use for others is the one that God will use for you.

We will be honored the way we honor God and others. In chapters six and seven, I talked about giving value to God's holy day and honoring it on a personal level. According to Luke 6:38b *we* decide the measure God is going to use for us. In other words, the measuring stick is in our hands.

As I wrote at the beginning of this chapter, there is a prophetic ring to this part of scripture. Do you dare to think about the promised blessings of honoring God's day on a small scale, a bigger scale, or even a worldwide scale? I have tried.

Local church scale

Let's say, as a church we will decide that from now on we will value the holy day and honor it in the way described by Isaiah. What will be the result? Well, apart from the extra time each person will gain and the joy that we will experience, the whole church will receive God's corporate blessing. The church will be honored and might set an example for many other churches to follow. People might come to us for advice and encouragement.

We might be invited to other churches to talk and help them to honor the Sabbath in a way that is a joy for everyone. We might exchange ideas and experiences.

Like I said before, I don't know exactly how God is going to do it, but I know He sure is capable of keeping His promise.

Christian scale

Do you dare to take this a step up? What if Christians (in a country) decided to start valuing and honoring a Sabbath day again? Millions and millions of people would gain extra time, would find joy, and would be honored all over the world.

Before I visited the USA for the first time, the only picture I had was what I had seen on television and in movie productions. To be honest with you, that was not a pretty picture. Hollywood didn't exactly do her best to make America honored all over the world. A portrait of sex, crime, drugs, and violence has been widely spread. Most of the time that is the only picture foreigners have of the USA. I remember when my parents came to visit us in California. During their stay, my father said almost every day: 'This is not how I pictured it.' He was totally taken by surprise at the beauty of the land and the friendliness of the people.

I grew up in the Netherlands and I know that the only picture many foreigners have, is the one of windmills, wooden shoes, prostitution in the streets, and legalized drugs. I talked to people who actually thought we drink tulip juice in Holland. Images are created by the media and they are often doing a poor job. The secular media only show us what they want us to see. In other words, we see a colored picture.

When God says that He can make us honored all over the world, we can be sure that He will do a better job than the mainstream media or even use the media to do a better job. Maybe the time has come to send out another picture of our societies, of the way we live. Christian communities in every town, city, and nation can indeed set an international example on how to honor God; it will be contagious. The time has come to get rid of negative and ungodly propaganda.

We need stories of people who have real joy in serving God, because they decided to start honoring His commands. This Christian movement could start in any country and spread all over the world. A Bible-based refreshment of Christianity with your country as the birthplace. Think about it. Don't you think God is able to honor believers all over the world again?

Nationwide scale

Wow, this kind of thinking asks for courage and maybe the ability to dream big. What if non-believers could see the change in the lives of those Christians who lovingly honor a Sabbath? What if they could see the peace, the joy, and the satisfaction? What if the government decided to change some rules? In the Netherlands Christians do not make up the majority of the population, but Sunday is by most people regarded as a day of rest. Stores, businesses, and shopping malls used to be closed. As a matter of fact they all used to close on Saturday at around six o'clock, and not open up until Monday midday. So, everyone could enjoy a real day of rest.

In general, there is less traffic on the freeways and many families spend their time together. It hurts me to see that rather quickly our society is changing and turning into a 24/7 chaos as well. Some cities decided to have shopping Sundays once or twice a month. Some stores stay open until Saturday evening at eight o'clock. I know this does not sound alarming to people who are used to a 24/7 society, but in the Netherlands it resulted in strong arguments and political debates.

As in many things, the USA is ahead. The godless tide is turning there. After removing the Ten Commandments from schools and courthouses, Louisiana is the first state to require to post the Ten Commandments in classrooms (June 2024). After removing prayer out of schools, the state of Oklahoma issued an order that every classroom should have a Bible and that teachers must teach from it (June 2024). I see that as a positive development. Not that we will go back to obeying the letter, but that we will learn to obey the Spirit.

Is it possible, as a nation, to turn from promoting a 24/7 society as the ultimate free lifestyle, to a society that finds her freedom in taking a day of rest after every six days of work? Is it possible to find more time by doing less? Is it possible to turn from a busy, busy lifestyle that many of us have adapted as normal, to a more peaceful and joyful life? Is there truly a way out of our hectic schedule?

Well, it doesn't hurt to admit that we made a mistake; it is not too late to turn back. Any nation could become an example of how God wants to make His children honored all over the world!

Meditate on the following:

- *If applicable, how do I feel when visiting other countries?*
- *What is the biggest thing that I have seen God doing?*

Journal your thoughts:

13

Enjoying the land

You should realize, then, that the real descendants of Abraham are the people who have faith.

Galatians 3:7

This is the part in Isaiah 58:14 that really stood out for me when I read it that morning, back in August 2004, at the breakfast table.

Then you will find the joy that comes from serving me. I will make you honored all over the world, <u>and you will enjoy the land I gave to your ancestor, Jacob.</u> I, the Lord, have spoken.

It answered a lot of my questions. As with most other verses applied in this book, I looked up the NIV and NKJV translations as well. The NIV translated it this way:

... and I will cause you to ride on the heights of the land and to feast on the inheritance of your father Jacob.

I would like to expand on this verse the way the Holy Spirit showed it to me and translated it into my present-day thinking.

When reading the Bible, I rely upon the guidance of the Holy Spirit, the same Spirit who inspired the authors at the time of writing, in order to understand what God wants to teach me. I simply ask God to open my eyes for His Word the way the Psalmist did, for example in Psalm 119:18,

Open my eyes, so that I may see the wonderful truths in Your Law.

Oh, have you ever prayed that? Open my eyes that I may see the wonderful truths in Your law. I did, many times. And I hope this book will help you to pray that prayer more often. It is necessary for our spiritual eyes and intellectual minds to be opened for the secrets of God's Word. Jesus did the same thing for the disciples as we can read in Luke 24:45. What a wonderful and powerful event:

Then He opened their minds to understand the Scriptures.

I can truly say He did the same thing for me when I came to faith. He opened my eyes and my mind for His Word. It was a turning point in the Bible and it surely was a turning point in my life. Jesus then told His disciples to wait for the power of the Holy Spirit to come down upon them. We know that after Jesus' departure it is indeed the Spirit that opens our eyes. 1 Corinthians 2:10 explains a bit more about the function of the Holy Spirit.

The Spirit searches everything, even the hidden depths of God's purposes.

A little bit further, in verse 12, the Bible explains why we have received the Spirit.

We have not received this world's spirit; instead, we have received the Spirit sent by God, so that we may know all that God has given us.

So that we may know all that God has given us. The Holy Spirit and the Bible are God's gifts to us. God wants us to meditate on his Word, to get familiar with it. It is the Holy Spirit who makes the Bible so interesting to read. I dare to say that He gives life and meaning to the words. No matter if we read it literally, practically, historically, spiritually, or symbolically, it is the Holy Spirit who will teach us the true depths of God's Word.

Jesus talks very plainly, yet so powerfully, about the work of the Spirit in John 14:26,

The Helper, the Holy Spirit, whom the Father will send in My Name, will teach you everything and make you remember all that I have told you.

What an awesome promise! The Bible, therefore, is a dimensional book. There is always a deeper side to it than we can see. The message is always powerful and the Spirit will teach us everything. That is why I would like to expand on the promise in Isaiah 58:14 to 'enjoy the land', as I understood it. Of course 'the land' as mentioned in this verse was Israël and not The Netherlands or the USA for that matter. But as we will see in the next few paragraphs, we could apply the promise to our own situation, to our own nation. However we look at it, the verse holds a promise, a blessing.

From 1989 to 2012 my husband and I have been visiting the USA on and off. We did a lot of traveling all over the world, with the mainland USA and California (as well as some neighboring states) as one of our favorite hangouts. It did not take long for us to figure out that the way we lived was not the so-called American way. We both worked seven or eight months a year in the Netherlands, saved up some money, and traveled the rest of the year all over the world. As a result of that, we never had permanent jobs, did not do career building, and certainly have no pension to look forward to.

We noticed that the common way of thinking in the USA is to work as hard and as much as we can, retire early, and then start enjoying life. Of course I write this with the notion that exceptions to the rule are always there.

We always thought this was kind of odd. Why postpone enjoyment of life until the day it might be hard to enjoy because of age or health issues? That did not make sense.

For years and years we absolutely enjoyed the beauty of America's many parks and nature reserves. We often said: 'God truly saw that it was good when He made America.' The country has been blessed with incredible nature, for us it is one of the most beautiful and diverse countries in the world.

Whenever we would rave about the beauty to someone in the store, at the gas station, or wherever, the response would almost always be: 'Well, you guys have seen more of this country than me.' A lot of people we've met had never been out of state. Now, we understand that not everyone has the desire to travel. Some folks are just downright happy to be at home. Nevertheless, a commonly used excuse is: 'I don't have time to travel now, I am working to pay my bills. Maybe one day when I retire, I am too busy right now.'

Thoughts about the American way of life were the first ones that came to my mind when I read the part in Isaiah 58:14 where God promises the people who treat the Sabbath as sacred the ability to enjoy the land. I know this scripture talks about the land that God gave to our ancestor Jacob, and I know that wasn't the USA, but let's take a look at Galatians 3:7.

You should realize, then, that the real descendants of Abraham are the people who have faith.

When the Bible talks about the real descendants of Abraham, and thus Jacob, the Bible is talking about the believers. Abraham, Isaac, and Jacob are our ancestors as well. So, why not personalize this and apply it to the land where we are currently living?

Is it possible that the reason why many people do not enjoy the land that was given to them, is the fact that they don't take a day of rest every seventh day and dedicate it to the Lord? Just make that verse personal for the country that you are living in at this moment.

Why would God make such an incredible, beautiful country for millions of people? To merely exist and work as slaves? To build houses just about everywhere? To pollute nature? Did He have a retirement community in mind when He shaped the Sierra's, when He formed the beaches, and when He created the forests? Do we think our excuses to postpone enjoyment of what He made for us, by about fifty years, will impress Him? Even if you are not an outdoors person, there are tons of possibilities to enjoy the land that was given to you, for example reading a book at the beach, having a family BBQ in the park, visiting a rose garden, anything!

Now, we may feel this is not what God had in mind when He spoke to the Israelites. We may even think this scripture has nothing to do with the way we live today. Well, the Bible certainly has to do with the lives we are living today. Think about it for a moment. We can make the Bible as personal as we want. As I wrote in the beginning of this book, don't read this with the word 'history' all over it. Apply it to your daily life. The Bible is God's living Word, it can and will speak to us today. If you read this scripture what thoughts come to your mind? How do you read it?

Be honest, do you enjoy the land, state, county, town, or house you live in? Do you appreciate its beauty, the space, the variety? Would you like to spend more time doing fun things but are you always busy? Have you been thinking about horseback riding, playing golf, kayaking, or starting a flower garden, but it seems you cannot find the time? Do you see where I am going with this?

If we start honoring and valuing God's holy day, we will always have enough time to get everything done. Not just enough time to get everything done, we will actually enjoy where we live and how we live. God clearly promises us the joy that comes from serving Him and enjoyment of the land we live in. Now, isn't that a comforting promise?

Meditate on the following:

- *Do I enjoy the place, whether it is my job, my home, my country, that God has given me?*
- *What natural and spiritual improvements do I want to see in my life?*

Journal your thoughts:

14

We encouraged you, we comforted you, and we kept urging you to live the kind of life that pleases God, who calls you to share in his own Kingdom and glory.

1 Thessalonians 2:12

So, let us think about those words one more time. Isaiah 58:14.

Then you will find the joy that comes from serving me. I will make you honored all over the world, <u>and you will enjoy the land I gave to your ancestor, Jacob.</u> I, the Lord, have spoken.

Personally, I believe that it is possible that people are not being able to enjoy where they live because they do not honor a Sabbath. I know this is a bold statement and I am glad the thought didn't come from nowhere. It is how I read that particular scripture in Isaiah 58 and it is what the Holy Spirit whispered in my heart. I could almost feel His pain about the stressful lives many people are living, not being able to enjoy where they are in life.

I realize, of course, that there are people everywhere who are downright happy where they live and how they live. I understand it is not possible to apply a scripture like this one to everyone and suggest that we are all struggling with the same issues. As I stated at the beginning of this book, God speaks to us personally but He also speaks to a nation that reads His Word. He speaks to a generation that is struggling with stress, burn-outs, and too little time to get everything done. I am sure you will know right in your spirit whether this is about you or not.

I just want all of us to think about our personal situations. Are we truly happy and satisfied where we live and how we live, or is there deep down inside that longing for change? If only I had more time. If only I had visited more countries. Very often we think that reaching our next goal will bring us closer to fulfillment of our dreams, but will there ever be an end to our feeling of lack? Is it possible to enjoy who we are, where we are, and what we are in life without having to add?

I believe, that when we start to honor and value His holy day we will discover that the rest of the week will be blessed as well. We will find joy in serving God and we will be able to truly enjoy where we live. We will be able to see God's hand in it all.

When God says that we will enjoy the land that He gave to our ancestor, Jacob, He is talking about the blessing as promised to Abraham, Isaac, and Jacob. Let's take a look. Just for context's sake. In Genesis 12:2 we can read about God's first promise to Abram (his name hadn't been changed yet).

I will give you many descendants, and they will become a great nation. I will bless you and make your name famous, so that you will be a blessing.

As Abram moved on with his life, God kept repeating His promise to him and later on to his son Isaac and his grandson Jacob. God spoke reassuring words again and again. Do not be afraid, Abram. I will shield you from danger and give you a great reward (Genesis 15:1). Abraham might have had many reasons to doubt God's goodness and purposes with his life, but he remained faithful.

Many years later his grandson Jacob was in great need to hear God speak again. In the 28th chapter of Genesis we can read about Jacob's famous stairway to heaven and encounter with God, who spoke very clearly to him,

Remember, I will be with you and protect you wherever you go, and I will bring you back to this land. I will not leave you until I have done all that I have promised you (Genesis 28:15).

One of the highlights of Jacob's story can be found in Genesis 35 where God blesses him again, just as He did with Abraham. Verse 11 and 12 are holding the promises.

I am Almighty God. Have many children. Nations will be descended from you, and you will be the ancestor of kings. I will give you the land which I gave to Abraham and to Isaac, and I will also give it to your descendants after you.

Nations will be descended from you, I find that very interesting. Many years passed and after the death of Jacob's son Joseph, the Israelites were treated very cruelly in Egypt where they were held in slavery. It was Moses who was called by God to rescue them out of slavery and bring them into the promised land.

Spiritually speaking, Egypt symbolizes our old, sinful life before we become believers. The promised land is the new life that we can have after being joined with Christ, also known as life in the Kingdom. Now, when God says that we will be able to enjoy the land that was given to us, He is talking about our natural *and* spiritual lives while being here on earth. The lives we live on a daily basis as well as the lives we received through our faith in Jesus Christ.

Isaiah 58:13-14 in other words tells us: when we obey God, He promises us an uplifting of our natural as well as our spiritual lives. We will actually feel at home in our land *and* in the Kingdom. It doesn't really matter how we read this scripture. A promise is a promise. We can take it spiritually, literally, or both. Ask the Holy Spirit to help you.

I hope and pray that by now you have a clear idea how to please God (Ephesians 5:10). Remember, we should not be pleasing God to get things done from Him or to become better people. We should be pleasing God because we love Him, because we respect Him, and because we are thankful for His love for us.

Remember when you were in love for the first time? You probably did the silliest things to please your love. You probably went out of your way just to be with that person. Maybe you listened to music together that you did not even like; maybe you saw movies together that weren't your choice. You didn't even care.

Nothing was too crazy to get her or his attention. Being in love with God means getting out of our way to please Him. Don't you think it is rather weird to say that we love the Lord and at the same time refuse to do what pleases Him? That would not work in human relationships. When we love someone we like to please that person, even if it was just to see a smile on their faces.

Treating the Sabbath as sacred is just one way of pleasing God. One way with many blessings attached. Of course

He gave us many ways to please Him. Think about the Ten Commandments as a whole, which of course are all summed up by Jesus in one new commandment. We can read so in John 15:11-12,

I have told you this so that my joy may be in you and that your joy may be complete. My commandment is this: love one another, just as I love you.

That pleases God!

__Meditate on the following:__

- *Do I love God? Do I want to please Him?*
- *A Sabbath day… how could it change my life?*

__Journal your thoughts:__

15

I, the Lord have spoken

When He spoke, the world was created

Psalm 33:9

Never before would I have thought it possible to write so much about just two verses in the Bible. It tells me something about the enormous impact of God's Word.

If just two verses give enough inspiration for a book, just imagine how many books are hidden in the Bible. People get inspired every day, all over the world, when they read God's Word. Reading about God must be like being with Jesus. The gospel of John ends with these words:

Now, there are many other things that Jesus did. If they were all written down one by one, I suppose that the whole world could not hold the books that would be written.

Wow, what a privilege to have walked and worked with Jesus. Every day must have been so exciting. If only we could have been alive when Jesus walked the earth.

When He performed miracles and taught His disciples how to pray. It would be so much easier to believe in all those things. Well, maybe Jesus doesn't walk the earth in human form right now, but He certainly still works miracles and teaches people through the Holy Spirit and the Bible. If we apply the Word of God in our daily lives it will be like walking with Jesus. It will be like having our teacher right there with us. 2 Timothy 3:16-17 says.

All Scripture is inspired by God and is useful for teaching the truth, rebuking error, correcting faults, and giving instruction for right living, so that the person who serves God may be fully qualified and equipped to do every kind of good deed.

Yes, as Christians we can be fully equipped to do our work if we use the Bible for guidance and direction.

That is why throughout this book I asked all of us to read the Bible as if God is speaking to us today. In other words, personalize what we read. The Bible may be an old book, but it is the only book that is truly alive, simply because God inspired it. God's Spirit is in it and God is eternal. He is not bound by time, what He said then, He says now. His words are truth, always! That is why we can apply old principles, sayings, wisdom, and teachings from the Bible in our lives today and they still work!

The Bible is our handbook for life and it is God's Word. We are supposed to do what it says, not just read it and forget about it. The Bible only works for us if we work it. Isaiah 58:13-14 ends with the words:

I, the Lord have spoken.

The NIV translation says it this way:

The mouth of the Lord has spoken.

'When the Lord speaks, He creates,' I wrote in chapter one. It is my hope that He spoke to your heart and that His words created a new desire in you to live according to His Word in your daily life.

The words that come from the mouth of the Lord are food for our spiritual lives. They will nourish and sustain us, like natural food nourishes our bodies. In Deuteronomy 8:3 (NIV) the Israelites learned that when they were on their way to the promised land, just eating natural food wasn't enough.

He humbled you, causing you to hunger and then feeding you with manna, which neither you nor your ancestors had known, to teach you that man does not live on bread alone but on every word that comes from the mouth of the Lord.

Yes, we need to feed our natural bodies in order to grow, stay healthy, and be strong. People with eating disorders know how true this is. Not eating, eating too much, or eating the wrong things will cause ailments, pains, and sickness. It will cause physical as well as mental imbalances. When not taken care of properly, the person could eventually die of these afflictions.

In the same way, we need spiritual food in order to grow spiritually. We cannot claim to be a Christian without having Jesus Christ in our lives, because without Him we won't be able to grow. Not growing means slowly dying. Jesus referred to Himself as the living bread in John 6:35,

"I am the bread of life," Jesus told them. "Those who come to me will never be hungry; those who believe in me will never be thirsty."

The Word of God is not only nourishment for our souls, but it is also a weapon against the enemy, Satan, who tries to steal, kill, and destroy our lives. Jesus used the same words from Deuteronomy 8:3 to refute the devil who wanted to trap and mislead Him. In Matthew 4:4 Jesus answers the devil with the following words:

The scripture says, 'Man cannot live on bread alone, but needs every word that God speaks.'

Note that Jesus says that we need every word that God speaks. God's Word nourishes our souls, resists the devil, and builds up our faith.

I pray and hope that while reading this book you have discovered the power of God's Word. God's Word is fulfilled in Jesus, that is such an awesome miracle. No other book in the Bible opens as powerfully as the gospel of John. No matter how many times I read it, it leaves me speechless. Just listen to verse 1:4,

In the beginning the Word already existed; the Word was with God, and the Word was God. From the very beginning the Word was with God. Through him God made all things; not one thing in all creation was made without him. The Word was the source of life, and this life brought light to people.

John 1:14 reveals that the Word was Jesus.

The Word became a human being and, full of grace and truth, lived among us.

All God's words were personified in Jesus. Everything God said was fulfilled in His Son. Earlier in this book we saw that God's laws are fulfilled in Him as well. Jesus showed us the way to a better life. Jesus is the way to a better life!

I have taken one of God's commandments out of its birthplace in history and put it in our daily lives at the dawn of the 21st century. I pray that keeping a holy Sabbath will change the way we live and that it will give everyone a bigger desire to please God. I do not have to prove that God's Word still works today; it will prove itself.

I like to end this book with the same words I opened with in chapter one, the words of Jesus in Matthew 13:9,

Listen, then, if you have ears!

Meditate on the following:

- *In what areas of my spiritual life did I grow last year?*
- *How can I treat God's Word as food for my soul?*
- *By what morals do I live?*

Journal your thoughts:

Pray aloud:

Dear Father in Heaven, thank You for keeping Your part of the deal, for promising me joy. Thank You for being a God that wants to bless me because You love me. I want to bless You because I love You! Thank You for overseeing the world. You know me; You know every single person on earth.

Holy Spirit, help me to keep my promises and help me to serve in many ways. I do not want to think of it as work, but as dedication and kindness. I ask You to change my attitude toward the commandments. Please, open my eyes for the Word so I can read it, love it, and live it. I ask You to help me to dream big; I can make a positive difference in an ever-changing world.

Dear God, I want to do it Your way. Thank You for giving me a new life. Thank You for promising me enjoyment of all You've given me. Most of all, I want to love You the way You love me. Holy Spirit, help me to set my goals and to be obedient.

In Jesus' name I ask this. Amen.

A Sabbath's Prayer

Lord, this is the day You have made
and I want to rejoice in it.

I want to value and honor this day because I love you.

I confess that I need to spend precious time with You.

May everything I do or say be pleasing to You.

My ears are open, speak to me please.

Amen.

Bibliography

Also available in English:

No other gods, *Why undivided loyalty to the One and only living God matters in these days (2023)*

The fierce lobby to remove biblical principles and standards from society has resulted in a generation losing touch with the core values of Christianity. This supplies a perfect base for the enemy to enter life as we know it. Major confusion, whether mentally, emotionally, physically, or spiritually, has become the epidemic of our time.

We have given the enemy, often by Supreme Court ruling, a free hand to do his thing… alienate people from the very God who created them. This alienation from God Himself and the values as described in His Word is not as liberating as expected. It opens the door for other gods. And they are here… plenty of them.

In this final book in the Ten Commandments series, we will be taking a closer look at the first commandment. 'You shall have no other gods before me' means so much more than just refraining from worshiping idols. It is a call for undivided loyalty towards the God of Israël and to honor Him as the supreme God, the Creator of heaven and earth. It is also a call to not be ignorant about the destructive influence of principalities and powers, demons and deities, false religious practices and forces of darkness.

We must decide now to stand up and take back what the enemy has stolen from us. Let's make it our aim to live life as God intended it, which is for us to be blessed and fruitful, content and encouraged, thankful and inspirational for generations to come.

First Love, *Embracing the challenge to pursue faithful relationships (2022)*

Love, till death do us part. Such words, promises, and vows… do they still mean anything at all in our world today? Is it possible to love and keep on loving? Is it possible to be faithful to the end?

Let's be honest, we have messed up big time when it comes to loving each other as human beings. We even messed up loving God. We have often failed to keep our promises, we have given in to temptations, and we have betrayed and hurt each other in many ways. Love has been replaced with lust, faithfulness with fantasy, and purity with perversity in our society today. This did not happen overnight, of course. It has been a slow decline of values and morals that were based on biblical principles and teachings.

When God said: 'Do not commit adultery', He was serious and He still is. Because our limited human love fails us, we need His divine love in our lives in order to be able to love others. It all starts with receiving His love, with renewing our understanding of that love, and with refreshing the way we love Him back. What God wants to establish in our spiritual lives, He will surely use in our day-to-day natural circumstances. After reading this book, you will:

- have a better understanding of God's love for people
- know that you are loved by God
- feel encouraged about refreshing your relationship with God, your spouse, and other people
- be inspired to love others as God loves you
- be able to ban boredom from your life
- be determined to remain faithful until the end.

True Worshipers, *Answering the father's call for a lifestyle of pure devotion* (2020)

2021 Illumination Book Awards Bronze Medal Winner
'Christian Living'

We never thought it could happen in just a few weeks, certainly not on a worldwide scale. But it did. Our churches had to close their doors, although temporarily, due to government regulations in response to a virus epidemic.

That brings us to a realistic and probing question. What would be left of our modern-day Christianity when all is taken away: the buildings, the meetings, the money, the power, the titles, the theology, the music, and the concerts? What would be left? We might find ourselves on our knees again, without anything. No effects, no band, no structure, no liturgy to follow. Just us, on the floor... waiting for God to speak, waiting for Him to come. After more than two thousand years of Christianity we might find ourselves bowing down again, empty-handed, with nothing but our time and lives to give Him.

Jesus prophesied that the time was coming when by the power of God's Spirit people would worship the Father as He really is, offering Him the true worship He so desires. Have you ever wondered what true worship would be like? It begins where idolatry ends. Yes, it will take a powerful move of the Holy Spirit to have our institutionalized Christianity make the transition into relational Christianity. And yes, this process starts in the heart of every believer. Will you answer the Father's call for a lifestyle of pure devotion?

In My Name, *Inviting God's holy presence in daily situations* (2018)

It is one thing to claim we don't use the Lord's name in vain, but what do we do? Are we bringing honor to His name? Do we have a genuine love for His name? And most of all, is everything we do and say then, done in His name? The letter of the Old Testament law says 'do not use the Lord's name in vain', Jesus however urges every believer to 'honor His holy name'. We will find out how such a commandment can become practical and applicable for believers today, not by focusing on what we cannot and should not do, but by focusing on what the Holy Spirit wants to do in us and through us. May we use God's name with power, purpose and reverence in effective ministry all over the world and in doing so be a generation that fulfills the ancient scriptures right here and now in the 21st century.

Spirit of Truth, *Finding certainty and standing firm in a troubled world* (2016)

One of the most famous questions ever asked in the history of mankind, was the one Pilate desperately confronted Jesus with: 'and what is truth?' In Spirit of Truth the reader is being challenged to answer Pilate's question and to go on a quest for that one certainty that would settle all dispute, all error, all doubt: Truth, with a capital T. Find out the importance of living and speaking truthfully and discover how to stand up for biblical values and principles in a troubled world that seems to have taken a free fall into lawlessness.

My Neighbor's House, *Digging Deeper to Find the Treasure That will Satisfy the Longing of Your Heart* (2013)

What do we do with the old pages of Exodus 20 in this current age and time? How do we apply them in our daily life? It is one thing to say, 'Oh, I don't envy my neighbor, his house, car, or wife. I don't desire what someone else has.' But come to think of it, what do you desire? What are the desires of your heart? Are you passionate for the right things? In this fifth book in the Ten Commandments series, you'll learn how to desire meaningful things and apply God's word to everyday life.

Grace of Giving, *Turning the Key to Enter & Experience Fullness of Life* (2011)

2011 Reader's Favorite Gold Medal Award Winner
'Best Christian Non-Fiction'

It is one thing to claim we do not steal, but the logical next question would be, 'What do we do? How do we go from merely obeying such a command to fulfilling it in our daily lives? Is it truly possible to become a cheerful giver?' In her award-winning book Grace of Giving, the fourth one in this series, Marja answers these questions by taking an in-depth look at the commandment 'do not steal.' The author offers a liberating and fresh insight on the eighth commandment as she shares how we can leave behind the way of the thief, which always cries for more, more, more. In her known step-by-step method, she slowly reveals the way of the Master, which is cheerful, abundant, and costly giving that will lead us into a life in all its fullness!

Breath of Life, *A Journey into Origin and Purpose of Spirit, Soul, and Body* (2008)

As human beings, we are made in the image and likeness of God. We are uniquely designed triune beings: spirit, soul, and body, yet one. The author takes the reader on a journey to our earthly beginnings and beyond. Based on biblical concepts and a surprising array of scriptures, she has painted an artistic picture of a colorful and loving God who is the source of all life. Breath of life is based on the commandment not to commit murder and it deals with the very core of our existence: life before and after conception.

Respectfully Yours, *Revealing God's Truth about Well-being and a Long Life* (2007)

Respectfully Yours is the second book in a series about the Ten Commandments in the twenty-first century. Based on the commandment to honor our parents, it deals with a much broader aspect of family life—the mutual respect between God, parents, and children. The letter of the Old Testament bursts into life as author Marja explains the new way of the Spirit. This book is not just a short and easy-to-understand study; it is a thought-

provoking page turner that will transform your view of
the parent-child relationship!

Visit the author at www.marjameijers.com